Katharine Hepburn

KATHARINE HEPBURN

A celebration by Sheridan Morley

Picture research by The Kobal Collection

PAVILION
MICHAEL JOSEPH

For Alexis

This edition published in Great Britain in 1989 by
PAVILION BOOKS LIMITED
196 Shaftesbury Avenue, London WC2H 8JL
in association with Michael Joseph Limited
27 Wrights Lane, London W8 5TZ

First hardback edition published in 1984

Designed by Lawrence Edwards

A CIP catalogue record for this book is
available from the British Library

ISBN 1 85145 352 0

10 9 8 7 6 5 4 3 2

Printed and bound in Great Britain
by Butler & Tanner Ltd, Frome

CONTENTS

'Play her like Eleanor Roosevelt'

1

IT WAS JOHN HUSTON WHO UNDERSTOOD IT FIRST, and all of thirty years ago on a film he was directing called *The African Queen*. My father was playing Hepburn's missionary brother, and as a child I was occasionally allowed onto the Shepperton set to meet her, which is why even now I find it impossible to think of her without immediately thinking of her in the context of that film. By the time Robert joined them for the studio scenes which open the film but were shot last, Huston and Bogart and Hepburn had been with the unit on location for two months in the Belgian Congo and it had not been an altogether easy or happy experience. Several of the crew went down with malaria, Hepburn herself caught a bad case of dysentery, spartan conditions sorely strained the long-established professional relationship between Huston (who loved Africa) and Bogart (who loathed it) and, worst of all, Hepburn seemed at first to have been totally miscast for Rose Sayer, the skinny churchmarm spinster who is taken by Bogart's Charlie Allnutt on board his ramshackle African Queen for a First World War journey down an African river. Indeed Bogart himself could hardly contain his early but deep distaste for his new co-star:

'She won't let anybody get a word in edgewise and she keeps repeating what a superior person she is. Later, you get a load of the babe stalking through the African jungle as though she had beaten Livingstone to it. Her shirt-tail is carefully torn for casual effect and is flapping out of her jeans. She pounces on the flora and fauna with a home-movie camera like a kid going to his first Christmas tree, and she blunders within ten feet of a wild boar's tusks for a close-up of the beast. About every other minute she wrings her hands in ecstasy and says "What divine natives! What divine morning glories!". Brother, your brow goes up . . . is this something from *The Philadelphia Story*?'

Bogart was clearly not about to emulate that other iron-jawed superstar of the old Hollywood, Spencer Tracy, in his devotion to Hepburn: but his animosity towards her might not have mattered (on screen it was after all to be a mainstay of the story) had it not been based on a feeling shared by Huston after a few days' shooting that Hepburn was totally wrong in the role. 'I told her that her interpretation of Rosie was doing harm to the picture as well as hurting the character. That her behaviour toward Charlie put her on a level with him, whereas she should consider Charlie so far beneath her that she treats him as a lady treats a servant.'

Hepburn thought about that for a moment and then asked her director if he had any particular lady in mind. Huston thought for a while. 'Eleanor Roosevelt' he said, 'play her like Eleanor Roosevelt.'

It was advice which was to echo far beyond the soundtrack of the movie. Hepburn did indeed play Rosie like Mrs Roosevelt, helped Bogart on towards the only Oscar he ever won and very nearly won one herself along the way (she was narrowly beaten by Vivien Leigh in *Streetcar*). But from that time forward, something of the notion of Hepburn as Roosevelt, of Hepburn as American royalty in fact, was to stay in the minds of her critics, interviewers, producers, directors and audiences alike. It wasn't that she, any more than Eleanor Roosevelt, could always be sure of a good press or even a successful year; but there was something about the way she was treated publicly, something about the space she was given to lead her own very private life, something about the respect she was gradually accorded, which was very royal indeed.

How else to explain the fact that in the heart of Hollywood, then the greatest gossip centre in the world, her thirty-year love affair with the married Spencer Tracy was treated as though it never existed? How else to explain the fact that when, early in 1981, a lady called Helen Lawrenson, whose career as a movie critic had started on *Vanity Fair* at about the same time that Hepburn was starting in films, published an article querying Hepburn's status as a major

screen actress, most better-known American film critics felt obliged to leap to her defence as though a Queen had been spat upon by a commoner?

Lawrenson's case was simple enough: Hepburn, she said, had won her two consecutive Oscars in 1967 and 1968 for nothing more than longevity. 'What she has always had is a photogenic bone structure, approximately two facial expressions (one haughty and the other when her eyes fill with tears, her chin quivers and she smiles tremulously) and a set pattern of vocal mannerisms, sometimes fascinating sometimes irritating, flaunted in that salt-and-vinegar voice of hers: strident, nasal, implacable as a dental drill.'

Miss Lawrenson was willing to concede that Hepburn had survived into her seventies with stamina, nerve and obstinacy: 'in her prickly way, she has exerted a legendary mesmerism'. What this veteran critic could not accept was the increasingly widespread press notion that Hepburn was a great or even a very good actress. Even here, however, the Lawrenson piece was forced to conclude that 'what Katharine Hepburn has always had is something perhaps even rarer than acting talent: a distinctive, tangy magnetism abetted by what the camera could make of her face and refuelled by remarkable ego and gumption. She has been affected and infuriating, but she has certainly not been boring.'

Not, certainly by normal critical standards, an especially savage attack and one that was originally made only to those who subscribed to an American Channel 13 magazine called *Dial*. Within weeks, however, it was brought to a vastly wider audience by the tremendous indignation of such fervent Hepburn supporters as Vincent Canby of the *New York Times* and Andrew Sarris of the *Village Voice*. Sarris indeed wrote of an 'enviously bitchy put-down by a venomous kiss-and-tell journalist', a far more waspish comment than anything achieved by Lawrenson herself on Hepburn.

But an icon had been attacked, and by the 1980s Hepburn had become critically sacrosanct in much the same way that, in the British theatre towards the end of her long career, Sybil Thorndike overcame all attackers by the simple device of outlasting them. Alone among native-born Hollywood stars Hepburn once actually led the Old Vic company, though admittedly only on a tour of Australia; alone among them she could probably have ended up, had she been born on the other side of the Atlantic, as Dame Katharine. Garbo and Monroe may have been more loved by the camera, and Davis and Crawford may have been more immediately responsive to its needs, but Hepburn alone brought to films a kind of distant, stagey, almost classical grandeur. Like Olivier in *The Entertainer* or Gielgud in *Arthur* or the dowager Queen Mary on a housing estate, she gave – and still gives – on screen a constant impression of greatness slumming, one all the more remarkable considering that her own background and pre-Hollywood stage career had hardly been either aristocratic or hugely distinguished.

What Hepburn understood however, before it became self-evident, was that Hollywood lived like Oscar Wilde's London on first and vague impressions. Without resorting to anything so coarsely obvious as press interviews, Hepburn managed to convey almost subliminally to producers and directors and co-stars and audiences alike that she came really from some other world and was only out in California on a visit of maybe twenty or thirty years. Back East (which in those pre-aviation days was a five-day rail trek) was where people believed Hepburn's real world lay; a world of triumphant Broadway stardom, suitors of unlimited wealth, cocktails of unimaginable sophistication: the world of Tracy Lord in Philip Barry's *The Philadelphia Story*, the play that everyone knew had been written for and about her, and maybe even partially by her as well.

It has been suggested that in Barry's story of the 'taming' of Tracy Lord by a journalist, and in her finally meek decision to remarry her first husband, there lies a kind of allegory about Hepburn going back to Hollywood on Hollywood's terms after the years in which she'd been labelled 'box-office poison'. But the Hepburn story, as opposed to the Tracy Lord story, had always been about survival rather than submission, and Hollywood always admired survival in an area where the professional mortality rate had been unusually high. By the time Hepburn began, in the late 1960s, to make it for the first time into the top ten box-office listings, she had been in movies for thirty-five years. Privately she had survived the death by hanging in childhood of a beloved brother, the crack-up of a first marriage, shortlived but much publicised affairs with Leland Hayward and Howard Hughes, then the years of secrecy about her love for Tracy, and his slow death. Professionally she had survived some terrible scripts and generations of box-office managers complaining to the studio chiefs that she was too classy for ordinary moviegoing audiences. Gradually though, while that craggy face began to look more and more as though it should have been carved into Mount Rushmore, Hepburn moved back to centre screen. Somewhere along the way she had ceased to be a problem for Hollywood and become instead one of its more splendid and powerful living legends. To find out how that metamorphosis was achieved, we had better go back to the very beginning.

15

'She seems to be borne up by light'

2

THE WOMAN WHOM PETER O'TOOLE ONCE FONDLY and memorably described as a combination of Medusa and Tugboat Annie was born Katharine Houghton Hepburn in Hartford, Connecticut on 8 November 1909. Like many actresses who decide to keep their birth-date a secret, she later paid the usual price of journalistic uncertainty which is that several reference books took a guess and ended up at 1907 instead of the truth, largely because Bryn Mawr records show her entering that school in 1924 and people expected her to be seventeen at that time where she was in fact barely fifteen. Hepburn however was giving nothing away: when her great friend and screen-writer Garson Kanin, shortly before he was banned from her presence for the unforgiveable sin of writing a book about her life with Tracy, finally lighted on her passport it was to discover that the birthday and birth-date she had inscribed there were in fact those of her late father, Dr Thomas Norval Hepburn.

He was, by all accounts, a remarkable man: one of the leading urologists of his time, he'd started out as a medical student and great athlete at college in Virginia and later Johns Hopkins, which was where he met one of the daughters of the formidably Bostonian Houghton family. Though proud enough of her family to give each of her own six children (including Katharine who was the second) the middle name of Houghton, Mrs Hepburn had rejected their more conservative traditions and had become instead a suffragette who picketed Woodrow Wilson's White House for women's rights and later proudly welcomed Mrs Emmeline Pankhurst into her home during an American tour. The Hepburns were thus regarded around Hartford with a mixture of curiosity and uneasiness: urology was not one of the medical callings that could openly be discussed in polite society, and Mrs Hepburn's passionate belief in militant feminism made her, too, something of a social outcast.

True, there was enough money to ensure a comfortable house in Hawthorne Street, and there was never much doubt that the children would go to the best schools in the East, among them of course Bryn Mawr which was where Kate acquired the accent later described by disgruntled cinema managers in less well-bred areas of America as that of a 'buzz-saw'. But it's important to realise at the outset that hers was very far from being the upper-crust Eastern-seaboard family immortalised by Barry in *The Philadelphia Story* and *Holiday*: the Hepburn family was not high society or even *High Society*, that final musical vulgarisation of Barry's classic script. Nobody much around the Hepburn household was for tennis, nor was marrying well high on any parental agenda. Rather they were a large, rebellious, intelligent family of achievers, in English terms more Chelsea or Hampstead than Mayfair; in later Hollywood terms Hepburn started out a lot closer to Jane Fonda than to Grace Kelly, only then to discover that she was being taken for the ice princess when she was really the tomboy rebel.

Hollywood's constant failure to come to terms with the real Hepburn stems from that early misapprehension about her background. She was never what they thought she must have been, and typically, although they ended up by showering her with no less than four leading-actress Oscars (an honour achieved by no other player), they were, with the one towering exception of *The Lion in Winter*, for relatively minor work – *Morning Glory*, *Guess Who's Coming to Dinner?* and *On Golden Pond*. And there you have some indication of the Hepburn that Hollywood wanted: either a stage-struck young waif (she was only twenty-four when she got that first Oscar for *Morning Glory*) or a lovable old harridan with a heart of gold and a voice of steel. The real Hepburn, the Hepburn who was neither of those celluloid clichés but an infinitely more complex and intriguing actress, was in fact the creation not of California but of Connecticut and Philadelphia and New York in the 1920s.

'My mother always brought me up to believe that women were never to be underdogs: she was a pioneer suffragist and an advocate of birth control and she taught me from a very early age that we were not necessarily the weaker sex. Apart from the freckles and the red hair that all my schoolfriends mocked, mine was a marvellous and secure childhood.'

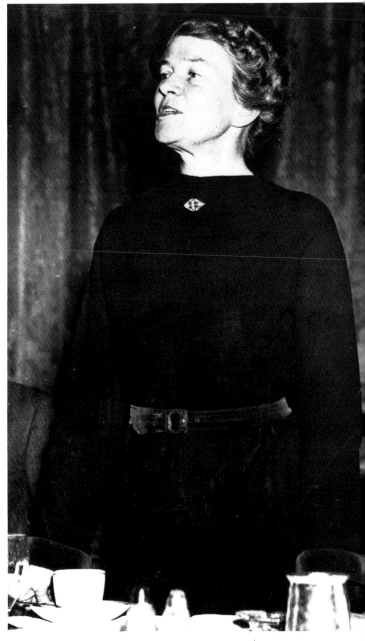

The Hepburns were a family keen on causes: soon after Katharine's birth her father happened upon a translation of *Damaged Goods* by Mrs Bernard Shaw and, after a lengthy correspondence with Shaw about the play's crucial importance in the fight against syphilis, took to sending it to some aghast colleagues at his hospital. His wife was, unusually for her time, an MA from Radcliffe and the family beliefs included free thinking, constant exercise and a passionate kind of sporting and tribal togetherness strongly reminiscent of the Kennedys.

And here too there was early tragedy: when Kate was ten, she and her beloved elder brother went to spend the Easter of 1920 with friends in Boston: on the Saturday night there was a party but when Kate awoke at her usual early hour the next morning and went down to breakfast, there was no sign of Tom. Searching around the house, she eventually found him hanging from one of the rafters in the attic: he had been dead for more than five hours.

Nobody, least of all the coroner, even suggested suicide: Tom had shown no signs of depression, indeed he had been the life and soul of the party the night before. There was, in the family view, only one appalling explanation

The Hepburn family home in Hartford, Connecticut: no liquor served, but Mrs Pankhurst once came to tea and conversational topics regularly included social hygiene, sexual relations, Marx, Fabianism and Shaw. 'We were a scandalous family; at any rate according to our more conservative neighbours.'

possible; a week earlier, Tom and Kate had been to the theatre to see a touring production of *A Connecticut Yankee at King Arthur's Court*. In that production, the dramatic highlight was the moment when the hero was to be seen apparently dead on stage, hanging from a tree with a rope around his neck. For a few days afterwards, Tom and Kate (who both were inclined to be more intrigued by backstage technique than great dramatic art) would discuss how it could be possible for an actor to hang himself on stage and then appear unscathed for the final curtain call. Tom, tragically, seems to have been trying to find out just that when he died.

In the view of Hepburn's best biographer, Charles Higham, the appalling discovery of her brother's body turned Kate overnight from 'an uncomplicated, open-faced, freckled, harum-scarum tomboy' into 'a highly nervous, moody girl suspicious of people, arrogant and disrespectful, bitter and hateful of religion. After seeing Tom dead, she no longer believed in a benign destiny or a life after death.' Mr Higham then goes on to speculate somewhat more fancifully that Hepburn's desire to be a movie actress may well have had something to do with a desire also to cheat death, to preserve herself on celluloid forever. The reality was I suspect a lot more prosaic.

After Tom's horrendous death, Kate began to look for some sort of escape from everything that reminded her of him: where once she had been happy to stay at the centre of a noisy, loving and close-knit family, she wanted now to withdraw into herself. Single children can do that whenever they choose: for a ten-year-old girl with still four younger brothers and sisters, escape was not so easy. If however she was to turn towards the theatre, which had always been Tom's childhood fascination as well as her own, and if she were to form her own children's theatre group, then she could play all the parts she chose – she could play little girls who had not just discovered their brothers hanging from rafters, and there would be her escape.

Within three months of her brother's death, Kate had formed the Hepburn Players: everything from *Marley's Ghost* to special amateur fund-raising performances of *Bluebeard* to benefit Navajo Indians was now the occupation of her childhood, and at Bryn Mawr she was to enter straight into college theatricals. She also won a bronze medal for figure skating one Christmas holiday at Madison Square Garden, got into the semi-finals of the Connecticut Young Women's Golf Championships, and swam and played tennis 'like a man'. She was in short the kind of teenager other girls resented, if only because she seemed so effortlessly able to survive in what was then still a man's world. She also seemed to have the utter confidence often found in the eldest survivor of a large brood of children: it was what others were soon to call arrogance.

Acting, particularly being the leading light of her own children's group (made up as often as not by the rest of her brothers and sisters plus the more amenable of their young neighbours), suited Hepburn in many ways: a compulsive organiser of other people's lives and activities, it gave her the chance to boss them around while doing something she was good at. The notion that here from childhood was a passionate and dedicated actress eager to explore her talent is highly implausible: years later she was to define acting as waiting around until somebody throws a custard pie in your face, and she always had far greater reverence for relatives who had become farmers than for neighbours in California who had become superstars.

Yet in the theatre she, like Sybil Thorndike and Gladys Cooper and Lilian Baylis back in England, found a place where even in the 1920s it was possible for a woman to dominate and by the time she got to Bryn Mawr, which had been her mother's old college, she was already reasonably certain that she was going to make her life in the theatre – for there was no question, coming from her family background, of anything but a career.

The Bryn Mawr college production of *The Truth About Blayds* **in 1927: Kate thinly disguised as a young man (second from right), discovering the truth also about her deep desire and apparent inability to act.**

Academically, Hepburn's career at Bryn Mawr was less than distinguished: astute teachers there however did her a deal, whereby the more her grades improved, the more college productions she would be allowed to act in. By the time she was eighteen she had therefore turned up in the chorus of college musicals (an experience to be drawn upon forty years later when she made her one and only appearance in a Broadway musical *Coco* as Coco Chanel) as well as *The Cradle Song* and Milne's *The Truth About Blayds* for which she was cast as a young man, experience that was again to prove useful when it came to the 1936 filming of Cukor's wonderfully eccentric transvestite romp *Sylvia Scarlett*.

And well before she had graduated from Bryn Mawr, she had already decided what she wanted to do for a living: in the Easter vacation

of her last year there, she wrote to Edwin H. Knopf, brother of the distinguished American publisher and who was himself later to carve out a Hollywood career as a producer at MGM. Knopf was at that time running a stock repertory company in Baltimore, and Hepburn wrote that she would be interested in working for him immediately she left Bryn Mawr that summer.

Knopf did not reply, Hepburn's letter being one of several dozen of its kind that even a local repertory producer could expect to receive in any given week. However even at eighteen she was not easily deterred and she then remembered something her father had taught her about making a way in the world: 'Go see people,' he had told her, 'never write to them; they can throw the letter in the bin but they can't throw you in the bin.' Borrowing the train fare from one of her earliest teenage admirers, Robert McKnight, later a world-renowned sculptor but at that time merely another of the Yale Art School students whom she had encountered at a Yale Prom, Hepburn arrived one morning in the office of a startled Edwin Knopf at the theatre in Baltimore.

His is therefore the first professional reaction we have to Hepburn's chances of future employment in the entertainment industry, and it is intriguingly similar to dozens of the verdicts of producers, directors, writers, co-stars and even box-office managers that were to dog her first twenty years or so in the American theatre and cinema. Knopf recalled 'a frecklefaced, bony, spindly girl with shocking red hair . . . an opinionated and brittle-voiced novice who was undoubtedly tremendously sincere but awkward, green, freaky-looking. I wanted no part of her.'

Knopf accordingly sent her back to Bryn Mawr with the suggestion that she might like to start thinking about some sort of career far away from the theatre; he was therefore more than a little aghast to find her back in his office three months later, on the morning after her graduation from Bryn Mawr. Knopf was then in mid-rehearsal with Mary Boland for a production of *The Czarina* and he had two options: he could either waste valuable rehearsal time on a second attempt to convince Hepburn that she was not cut out for an acting career, or he could cast her in the small not to say almost totally invisible role of a lady-in-waiting and hope that in due course she would make the discovery herself. ·

He took the easy option, gave her the role and dropped her thereby into one of the most serious rows she was ever to have with her family; Dr Hepburn took the view that it was all right to make an exhibition of yourself in some good cause, be it women's suffrage or the need to improve public knowledge of urine diseases. What was not all right was to make an exhibition of yourself merely in the name of

entertainment: that in his view was vanity and to be urgently discouraged. Even he however, having made those opinions known, gave her fifty dollars, told her there would be no more where that came from but wished her well in Baltimore. And it was there, a few weeks before her nineteenth birthday, that Katharine Hepburn made her professional stage debut in the summer of 1928.

The Czarina was only scheduled to run a week, during which time Mary Boland in the title role made two discoveries about her lady-in-waiting: one was that Hepburn never took her eyes off her, the other that when you costumed and lit Kate she went in an instant from ugly duckling to swan: she seems, noted Boland prophetically, 'to be borne up by light'.

*'A tougher and more
dynamic Peter Pan'*

3

HEPBURN STAYED WITH THE KNOPF COMPANY IN Baltimore for one more show in that summer of 1928 – another Mary Boland vehicle from Broadway called *The Cradle Snatchers* in which she had another walk-on role. Knopf was still sure she was never going to make it as an actress, and back in Hartford Connecticut her family were still hoping that this late teenage fling was soon going to end and that Kate would then settle down to a serious career: medicine, maybe, like her father, or even the law.

There was however one man who thought there was just a very faint chance that she might make it as an actress: Knopf's company stage manager at that time was Kenneth McKenna, who himself had been an actor for a while and was to end up years later as a distinguished head of the story department at MGM. McKenna realised that the first thing to be dealt with was the voice: breathy, untrained and nasal, it was the most obvious of the many hurdles that were to be overcome if Hepburn was ever to be made to seem anything but awkward on stage. And he knew, in New York, of a lady called Frances Robinson-Duff – a legendary voice coach whose other pupils over the years included Helen Hayes, Cornelia Otis Skinner, Ruth Chatterton, Ina Claire, Miriam Hopkins, James Stewart and the young Clark Gable.

Not a girl to waste much time, Kate moved to New York the moment *The Cradle Snatchers* run came to its end: her father grudgingly gave her enough money to rent an apartment and pay Miss Robinson-Duff ten dollars a lesson, and with what little she had left over she also took some dance and movement classes from Michael Mordkin. Learning her trade for a year or so in New York, then as now the heart of the American theatre, would not have been a bad idea for Hepburn. Events however moved rather faster than that. Only a month or two after she settled there, she learnt that Knopf had folded the company in Baltimore and was now intent on bringing into New York a new play called *The Big Pond* in which McKenna was playing the lead. Hepburn auditioned for them again, and this time was given the small role of a secretary as well as the task of understudying the star role, that of a rich American debutante who falls unsuitably in love with a mysterious Frenchman (McKenna). The play was being rehearsed and given its out-of-town tryout at Great Neck on Long Island and it was there, about a week before the first night, that Knopf on a curious impulse decided to sack his leading lady and give the role to Hepburn whom nine months earlier he'd been unwilling to let even into a Baltimore stock company.

Unsurprisingly, the first night in Great Neck was a total fiasco: Hepburn panicked at her first sustained contact with an audience, played the part faster and faster so that the third act deteriorated into an incomprehensible gabble and was fired from the show early the next morning. 'In those days,' she told Charles Higham, 'I was always getting fired from shows. I was what they called a "flash actor" . . . I could read well at auditions, laugh and cry and always get a part quickly, but then I could never keep it. I would lose my voice, get red in the face, talk too fast and I just couldn't act. The sight of people out there used to petrify me.'

After *The Big Pond* she went back to New York and made her Broadway debut at the Martin Beck on 12 September 1928 as 'a hostess' in an undistinguished flop called *Night Hostess* from which she also got sacked for looking, in the words of producer John Golden, 'altogether too wholesome'. From that she got into something called *These Days* which lasted all of eight nights but did lead on to her first real break. The producer of it, Arthur Hopkins, was also opening a new Philip Barry comedy called *Holiday* and decided that Hepburn would make an ideal understudy for Hope Williams in the starring role of the poor little rich girl Linda Seton who decides at the last minute to break away from her family's New York mansion for love of an impractical young adventurer. And Hope Williams, though unknown to Holly-

The Big Pond, **in summer stock at Baltimore, from which Kate was ignominiously dismissed after only one performance.**

wood or European audiences, was an almost perfect role model for the later Hepburn: an actress of extreme wealth and patrician elegance, she ventured occasionally onto Broadway when the mood took her and turned in light-comedy performances of considerable charm. Her devotion to the business of being an actress was however less than all-consuming: indeed when she heard that Hepburn was to be her understudy, she told her that if at any time Kate felt like actually playing the part, she had but to say so: Miss Williams would then be only too happy to find a social engagement for the evening and leave the spotlight to her.

Hepburn however had other ideas: after two weeks of understudying in *Holiday*, the role that was a decade later to give her one of her most archetypal and stylish screen hits, she announced that she would be leaving the company to go to Bermuda. On honeymoon.

Her only-ever marriage was early, hasty, shortlived and to say the least curious: indeed it seems to have made so little impression on

Hepburn herself that she often genuinely appeared to have trouble in recalling it when asked by journalists to recount the story of her life. The husband was Ludlow Ogden Smith, a wealthy French-educated Philadelphia socialite whom she had only known a few months, though long enough to bully him into changing his name to Ogden Ludlow so that she would never have to be known as Mrs Smith. By all accounts he was a man of extreme patience and devotion, willing at Kate's behest to abandon his close family and professional ties to Philadelphia and settle instead into a New York stockbroking firm so that his future wife could maintain her Broadway career. In fact he needn't have bothered: two months after their return from honeymoon. Kate was in the office of Arthur Hopkins asking to be re-employed as Hope Williams's understudy in *Holiday*. The marriage was over, though as neither of them much wanted to marry again they were not in fact divorced until May 1934. Quite why it ever happened in the first place remains unclear:

there are those who say Hepburn was desperate to escape the drudgery of being a Broadway understudy, but even by her impetuous standards marriage seems a drastic way of leaving a show. Certainly she and 'Luddy' were devoted to each other, and remained close if platonic friends across the next half-century; maybe it was just that Kate's lifelong passion for experiment, coupled with a certain puritanical streak, led her to try out what would now be an affair but what then had by her and her time's standards to be a full-scale marriage.

At any event it seems to have done neither party much lasting damage, and Kate even found a certain usefulness in being for years afterwards 'Mrs Ludlow' rather than just another unmarried actress roaming the streets of New York in search of work: the married name at least held at bay some of her more undesirable suitors, and gave a certain distance to the beginnings of the Hepburn image. She stayed with the *Holiday* company until it closed on Broadway in the late Spring of 1929, even playing a couple of performances for a genuinely indisposed Hope Williams. The Theatre Guild, later to be her most constant Broadway supporters, then offered her a small role in a Lunt-Fontanne comedy which she would have been well-advised to accept. Instead, she took a more tempting offer: a leading role opposite Philip Merivale in *Death Takes A Holiday*, a curious little fantasy about Death arriving in an Italian palazzo and eventually carting off its most glamorous occupant. Hepburn lasted in that role for about a fortnight in Philadelphia before being sacked by the management: by now she was getting used to it, however, and her father took the reassuring view that it was because she looked far too hale and hearty a girl to be carried off by Death.

Back in New York, the Theatre Guild were by now auditioning for *A Month in the Country*; its director was a young Russian soon to make his first movie – Rouben Mamoulian: 'So this

Mr and Mrs Ludlow Ogden Smith in 1928: 'Was I ever married? I really can't remember. It certainly wasn't for very long.'

Hepburn on stage, with George Colouris in *The Torch Bearers* (Berkshire Playhouse, Stockbridge, 1930) and with Leon Quartermaine in *Art and Mrs Bottle* (Broadway, 1930) which, said the drama critic of the *New York American* 'uncovers a young actress whose performance last night should raise her to stardom.' But it didn't, not for another couple of years at any rate.

girl came to see me and in walked a thin, slim figure with red hair, tightly combed back, freckled face, shaking and very nervous. Obviously very inexperienced: yet there was something there, a kind of luminosity about the face.'

But apparently not enough: Hepburn didn't get the role even of the maid, though she was allowed to step into it after the original actress left the cast a couple of months later. Some indication of how little impact she had made after eighteen months in the New York theatre can be gained from the fact that she appeared on all Theatre Guild posters and programmes as Katharine Hapburn.

Intriguingly, those who had thus far been most perspicacious about Hepburn (the actress Mary Boland and the director Mamoulian) had talked about her in purely filmic terms: a 'luminosity' about the face, a feeling that she was 'borne up by light'. Ten, even five years later it would have occurred to almost anybody that her logical place was therefore Hollywood rather than Broadway. But in 1930 Hollywood was only just beginning to go over to non-silent shooting, and the idea of a 'legit' actress from the East making a serious career out in the Californian sun was still laughable. Hepburn had not gone through Bryn Mawr to end up as the educated answer to Clara Bow.

Accordingly she struggled on in a theatre which seemed to have remarkably little interest in her admittedly eccentric stage presence: following *Month in the Country* she went off into summer stock at the Berkshire Playhouse at Stockbridge in Massachusetts with a fellow-pupil from her New York acting school, the American Express heiress Laura Harding. Others in that remarkable 1930 summer season included such later Hollywood character actors as George Colouris and Robert Coote, and Hepburn does seem to have lasted there long enough to learn the basic stage techniques which had so far proved elusive. At any rate as soon as the season closed she landed the ingénue role in *Art and Mrs Bottle*, a Benn Levy

comedy which was being produced on Broadway by Joseph Verner Reed:

'Each day streams of new applicants arrived: none of them would do, and when finally we did manage to select three possible candidates they were all rejected by the star, Jane Cowl, as unsuitable. Slamming her dressing-room door, Miss Cowl retired with the ultimatum that she would resign unless a suitable girl was selected within twenty-four hours. Disconsolately I sat alone on stage during the lunch hour, racking my brains trying to think of a suitable girl. I looked up and saw a young woman approaching. She couldn't have been an actress, she must have come on some other business. She wore tweeds and an outlandish hat; she was tall and slim and gawky; she looked, as though she might be good at high hurdles . . . Inwardly I groaned. Her voice, slightly rasping, invoked two-hundred-yard drives and brisk walks in the rain. But then, suddenly, I really saw her – she was as rare, as untrue to life and as moving as

a Primitive. She began to read. She didn't seem very good and yet, in a way, she was fascinating. She was like Alice in Wonderland only more firm, more angular, and she had Alice's youth and disarming honesty. Brusque, gallant somehow; and better still she was plain. Jane was delighted. She had found just the foil she was looking for. Everybody else thought she was terrible. Hideous to look upon, with a jarring voice, unschooled and clumsily tense; when Benn Levy laid eyes on her he reeled: "Why, she's revolting: and she's got Vaseline on her face, her skin glistens. No allure, impossible. Out with her".'

For the next four days of rehearsal the battle raged. Cowl and Reed pro-Hepburn, Levy as author leading the rest of the company in a determined attempt to get her out of the theatre. Eventually and predictably it was Kate herself who solved the dilemma by approaching Reed with her still-unsigned contract and an ultimatum: either he sign her there and then for

a run of the play, or she would not be turning up to rehearsals again. Courageously, Reed signed only then to find even Jane Cowl blaming him for hiring an untalented amateur. In a rehearsal period of quite remarkable confusion even by contemporary Broadway standards, fourteen other actresses were tried out in the role until a kind of weary general consensus agreed that Hepburn had by now gone further down the path than any of the others and had better be allowed to open since there was a press night less than a couple of weeks away.

And Hepburn did already have one great supporter in the cast: the young English actress Joyce Carey, daughter of Lilian Braithwaite, was then working in New York and became the first of Kate's many admirers from within the British theatre: stage-trained actresses from a 'legit' background who seemed always to understand something about Hepburn which confused and often defeated her American audiences. 'The great thing about Katharine Hepburn,' Miss Carey told me more than half a century later, 'was that she had class: she came from a rather higher drawer than anybody else I had met in New York. She wore no make-up, had her hair scraped back into a sort of bun and always wore a little bit of felt tied around her neck as if she was ashamed of its length. She was rude, anxious, grand: all qualities acceptable in a star but somehow surprising in somebody who was barely hanging onto a role for which most of the rest of the cast thought she's been badly miscast. But soon I got to know her and learnt that she didn't mean to be rude at all, she was just desperately shy and uncertain. She looked eccentric and somehow very like a star. I thought she was wonderful.'

Miss Carey was, however, well used to larger-than-life theatrical eccentrics, not least her own mother: New York lacked London's history of staginess and Hepburn was still putting up backs all over Broadway. Then however came the first night, her first-ever solo bow, and reviews which, while lukewarm for both Cowl and the play, were at least not so disastrous for Hepburn: 'agreeable to look at, assured and altogether proficient' thought the *Times*, though the *News* found her 'altogether too gangling and affected to play a romantic heroine'.

Art and Mrs Bottle stumbled through the Depression winter of 1930–31, playing in repertoire with a none-too-successful *Twelfth Night*, and when both productions ground to a halt early in February, Kate went back to Mrs Robinson-Duff for a little more theatrical instruction before going into summer stock at Ivorytown, Connecticut. Here as at Stockbridge the summer before (and Baltimore in 1928), she seemed to thrive and develop: something about those early summer seasons, away from the hothouse intensity of Broadway, suited her very well indeed. Summer stock was an altogether different existence, roughly corresponding to an adult version of the summer camps that have always been a part of affluent American teenage calendars. Shows were often rehearsed and staged on a weekly basis, but there still seemed to be time to swim and ride and lead the kind of outdoor life Hepburn loved best. Also of course she was given a range of work (the Ivorytown season featured *Cat and the Canary*, *Just Married* and *The Man Who Came Back*) rather than having to fight for a single role and then fight some more to retain it through rehearsal. Above all, Ivorytown was not far from the Hepburn summer cottage at Fenwick and therefore escape back to that ever-loving family was always possible when she tired of the green room conversations – as often she did. In fact from Hepburn's point of view, the only thing wrong with summer stock was that it ended with the summer, forcing her back to the indoor, neurotic and vastly less welcoming world of another Broadway season. This time though, she seemed at last to have struck lucky: the writer of *Holiday*, Philip Barry, had a new comedy called *The Animal Kingdom* for which he persuaded the producer Gilbert Miller to cast Hepburn opposite a young London

stage star out in New York en route for Hollywood – Leslie Howard. Rehearsals then took their usual stormy course: Howard loathed Hepburn, thought she was both too tall and too arrogant, finally decided her mannerisms were unbearable and managed after a week to have her replaced by Frances Fuller. That the play went on to give Mr Howard a considerable stage and screen success did nothing for Hepburn's confidence, and after her abrupt dismissal she briefly but seriously thought of abandoning the stage altogether. Here she was, now all of twenty-two but with five years in the business already behind her, and almost nothing to show for it except a series of short runs and stormy backstage dismissals: whoever said she had to be an actress anyway? More intelligent than most, and less obsessively ambitious to be a star, she was alert enough to realise that there was a world beyond Broadway, a world of medicine and the law and half a hundred professions to which women were now cautiously being admitted with a lot less of the heartache she had already endured in the theatre.

But only a month after her dismissal by Leslie Howard, the offer that kept Hepburn in the acting profession and indeed led directly to her movie stardom came from a somewhat unexpected quarter. A leading Chicago hosiery manufacture called Harry Moses had decided for reasons best known to himself that he wished to become a Broadway impresario, and to start his new life by staging an update of *Lysistrata* called *The Warrior's Husband*. Perhaps because tall and formidable women were not exactly thick on the Broadway ground, his eye rapidly fell on Hepburn for the leading role of Antiope, a character whose first entrance required her to leap down an entire flight of stairs while carrying a dead deer over her shoulders.

Whether because she thought this might well be her last chance to crack Broadway, or just because she recognised in Antiope a lady

'Miss Katharine Hepburn' (here with Colin Keith-Johnstone in the 1932 Broadway *Warrior's Husband*) 'as the young Amazon Antiope is a boyish, steel-sprung woman who suggests a tougher and more dynamic Peter Pan.' *New York Herald Tribune*

rather further up her street than the usual run of simpering juvenile romantics, Hepburn approached *The Warrior's Husband* as if training for a prize-fight. Inexhaustibly energetic, she virtually kidnapped the production from a drowsy director (Burk Simon) and ran with it to such an extent that, though only third-billed to Romney Brent and Colin Keith-Johnstone, she took the first-night audience by the storm of solo stardom. 'A tougher and more dynamic Peter Pan' thought the *Herald Tribune* while in *World Telegram* Robert Garland raved, 'Ever since she supported Jane Cowl in *Art and Mrs Bottle*, I've been waiting for Miss Hepburn to

fall heir to a role worthy of her talent and beauty. Antiope is that role . . . It's been many a night since so glowing a performance has brightened the Broadway scene.'

In spite of reviews like those, *The Warrior's Husband* only survived eighty performances on Broadway; adaptations of *Lysistrata* then as now being something less than a wow at New York box-offices. At one of those eighty performances however was a lady called Lillie Messenger, then employed as the New York talent scout for David O. Selznick at RKO Pictures, and within a month of the show's closing Hepburn had acquired an agent, Leland Hayward, and two screen tests.

'Did we stick David
fifteen hundred for that?'

4

THE ACTRESS WHO WAS IN LATER YEARS TO MAKE movie history by winning an unprecedented three and then four leading-actress Oscars did not arrive in California in anything remotely resembling a cloud of glory, nor was she trailing many such clouds from Broadway. True, the play that she was later to refer to dismissively as 'that leg show' had at last given her some sort of a reputation in New York, but *The Warrior's Husband* proved less than durable although it did serve to get Hepburn her first mention in *Time* magazine which referred in error and passing to 'a blonde, thin-cheeked girl' who might be worth watching on more interesting occasions.

That, too, was the opinion of Lillie Messenger, who wired Selznick on the coast with the news of a Broadway 'discovery' well worth testing. As it happened, another Hollywood director had already shown some interest in Kate: after the first night, John Ford had briefly thought of filming *The Warrior's Husband* and so tested its original cast. He soon abandoned the idea, however, and it was left to Miss Messenger to arrange Hepburn's first appearance in front of a camera. She knew, though Kate did not, that there was one particular film about to go into production at RKO for which Hepburn might well be suited. This was *A Bill of Divorcement*, Clemence Dane's old London stage play about the daughter who abandons her own future happiness in order to take care of the once-great but now mentally ill composer who is her father. This somewhat creaky but immensely serviceable vehicle had started out in 1919 as a novel called *Legend*: it had then been staged with Meggie Albanesi and filmed (with Fay Compton in 1922) before being produced on Broadway where it had made the name of another great Katharine, Cornell.

Now, Selznick was about to shoot the first talking version and the role of Sydney Fairfield was reckoned to be a considerable prize: front-runners for it were generally thought to be Norma Shearer, Irene Dunne and Anita

Louise, though there was already one dark horse, Laurence Olivier's first wife, Jill Esmond, who had gone out to Hollywood with him after their Broadway success in *Private Lives*. Despite this wealth of choice, Selznick's meticulous passion for exploring every conceivable avenue (one which was to be echoed a decade later in his endless search for a Scarlett O'Hara) led him to order a test on Hepburn the moment he had Miss Messenger's first report. By now, John Barrymore had already been cast for the role of the composer father, and a young George Cukor fresh from his first success with *What Price Hollywood?* had been hired to direct. Hepburn, even had she known of this glittering line-up, would probably have remained resolutely unimpressed: she hadn't cared for her one Hollywood contact with John Ford, especially after he had made it clear he would prefer Elissa Landi to play her *Lysistrata* role. She had no particular desire to leave New York or the legitimate theatre, and she regarded it as all too typical of Hollywood that they had only begun to express any interest in her when she had started to remove some clothing in *The Warrior's Husband*.

She would therefore have turned down RKO's request for a test, had it not been for Leland Hayward who had also seen her in the play and had by now become her agent; later the relationship was to turn even more serious than that. He persuaded Kate that a test could do no real harm and she then agreed, subject to three conditions – that she be allowed to choose the scene and the actor she would play opposite, and that he would be filmed only from over the shoulder. She had, she said, heard of too many actresses making tests with 'stooges' only later to find that it was the stooges who were given the contracts.

The scene she chose for the test was one from that most favourite of all her plays, even though she had as yet never managed to star in it: Philip Barry's *Holiday*. The actor she chose was Dorothy Parker's husband Alan Campbell, a

Broadway friend from *The Warrior's Husband* who promised to offer no competition, even with his back to the camera as agreed. Unlike most stage actresses suddenly asked to test in unfamiliar material and company, Hepburn had thus ensured that it was she who was on home territory here and the camera that was for once on trial.

And the result, recalled Cukor forty years later, 'was quite unlike any test I had ever seen before. Though she'd never made a movie, she seemed to have this very definite knowledge and feeling right from the start.'

There and then, Cukor and Selznick decided that they had to have Hepburn for *A Bill of Divorcement*: the bad news was broken to Jill Esmond, who returned to England and a subsequent divorce from Olivier. It was to be his second wife, Vivien Leigh, who a decade later wrested the role of Scarlett O'Hara from Hepburn for Selznick's *Gone With The Wind*. But despite the enthusiasm for her now, Hepburn was still deeply unsure that she particularly wanted to go to Hollywood. Largely to test their enthusiasm for her, she told Hayward to ask for fifteen hundred dollars a week from RKO, a sizeable sum since she'd only been getting a hundred a week for *The Warrior's Husband* and rather less than that when the business fell off and the company were asked to take cuts. Urged on by Cukor, Selznick offered twelve hundred and fifty: Hepburn refused, but Hayward (ever the perfect mediator) suggested that if paid fifteen hundred a week for the four weeks of shooting, his client might be prepared to throw in a week of free rehearsal. Faces were saved all around, and contracts were duly signed – despite the fact that in the meantime Hepburn had agreed to do a couple of weeks in her beloved summer stock at Ossining with a new play called *The Bride The Sun Shines On*.

Accordingly it was on 1 July 1932 that Hepburn finally boarded the Stratoliner train that was to take her in five days and nights across America to Los Angeles. For protection in a community she already viewed as at the back of beyond and probably foreign, she took her great friend Laura Harding. Both women were appalled by the heat, which they seem not to have known about, and as Kate stepped off the train at Pasadena in a rumpled skirt nursing a swollen eye which had become infected en route, Leland Hayward's California partner, the agent Myron Selznick who also happened to be the brother of her new employer, was heard to gasp 'My God, did we stick David fifteen hundred a week for that?'

Others were equally appalled, as David Selznick himself later noted: 'When Hepburn first appeared on our RKO lot there was consternation. "Ye Gods, that horse face" they cried, and when the first rushes were shown, the gloom around the studio was so heavy you could cut it with a knife.'

Nor were matters much helped by Hepburn's first encounter with her co-star: studio gossip was later, and inaccurately, to allege that he advanced on her stark naked, and though this, like so many other Barrymore stories needs to be regarded with suspicion, it is true that at first Hepburn's nervousness failed to endear her to the great man. Indeed his biographer Gene Fowler notes that after one particular studio row she threatened never to act with him again, to which Barrymore retorted that so far she hadn't anyway. But he was already at the start of his long and tragic decline, while she was simply starting at the top. Though she was only billed third to Barrymore and Billie Burke, it is clear from the very first appearance of her character on screen – a long tracking shot during which in silence she crosses an upstairs landing and slowly descends a staircase to join a party – that Cukor already knew precisely what he was doing with Hepburn: he was introducing a major new star to her first world-wide audience.

Selznick noted a sudden change in his studio's attitude to Hepburn at the very first private preview of *A Bill of Divorcement*.

'During the first few feet you could feel the audience's bewilderment at this completely new type, and also feel that they weren't quite used to this kind of face. But very early in the picture there was a scene in which Hepburn just walked across the room, stretched her arms and then lay out on the floor before the fireplace. It sounds very simple, but you could almost feel (and you could definitely hear) the excitement in the audience. It was one of the greatest experiences I've ever had. In those few simple feet of a film a new star was born.'

Others, including Kate herself, were still not so sure: though she had by now become very fond of Barrymore ('he shoved me before the cameras and taught me all that could be poured into one greenhorn in that short time') she didn't much care for Hollywood or a somewhat gloomy apartment she had rented with Laura Harding. 'It was so very depressing,' said one of their earliest visitors, Greta Garbo, 'but then of course I have always loved depressing things.' The moment that the four-week shooting was over Hepburn departed for a European summer vacation, taking her husband with her for old times' sake.

'She has dignity and an instinct for underplaying emotion, talents which are as rare in a film actress as they are novel. In her ability and good looks, Miss Hepburn has the makings of a star. All she needs is a little more familiarity with the microphone, some worthy roles and a firm determination not to let her producers exploit her as a second Garbo or a second Joan Crawford or a second anything.' *New York Post*

Selznick had already made it clear that he intended to exercise his option and keep her at RKO, though on her side of the contract Kate had a guarantee that for seven months of the year her life would be her own. By the time she and Ogden Ludlow got back from Europe, the early reviews were already coming in on *A Bill of Divorcement* and seemed to bear out Selznick's enthusiasm. The actress whom Cukor had once described as 'looking like a boa constrictor on a fast' had hit Hollywood at a time of characterless, synthetic blondes: 1932 was also the year of *As You Desire Me*, *Trouble in Paradise*, the original *Scarface* and *I Am A Fugitive From a Chain Gang*, but the number of remarkable actresses around California were few and far between, and the leading ladies on RKO's roster were Irene Dunne, Ann Harding and Constance Bennett so the competition there was not exactly intolerable.

Other studio rosters were not a lot better, though this was an admittedly very theatrical time when the movies, having only just learnt to talk, felt briefly obliged to photograph stage plays. The fight for the leading-actress of the year in the Oscars thus involved Lynn Fontanne, Helen Hayes and Marie Dressler: Hepburn like them was Broadway-based, but she already had something accidentally and crucially extra. The camera, as directed by the ultimate 'woman's director' George Cukor, both loved her and let audiences see that love. Where Fontanne and Hayes were soon back on Broadway, Hepburn was in Hollywood to stay.

A few weeks later, she gave her first long interview to a local fan magazine, one which noted that 'on the strength of a single picture, which was meant to be John Barrymore's anyway, Miss Hepburn is a young stranger already raised to Garbo's vacated throne.'

Hepburn herself was more prosaic. 'Sidney Fairfield in *A Bill of Divorcement* is an actor-proof part. Nobody can ever help being good in it. Katharine Cornell became a star on Broadway playing it, and the girl who did it in

England, Meggie Albanesi, died two years later but is still spoken of as a genius because of it. Nobody has ever been bad in that part. I wish people would wait until I've done another picture or two before they start to judge me. No one knows yet whether I'm good or bad, not even me. When I first arrived here, I didn't want to see anybody because I was sure I was going to turn out to be a flop, and I thought in that case the fewer who knew I'd been here at all the better. But then Mr Cukor and Mr Barrymore made the picture a lot of fun for me to do, though even so on the night of the first preview I caught a train back to New York so I wouldn't have to meet people who had seen it.

'People out here seem to think that I'm a millionairess and already much-married, but a very few of the things that have been printed about me are true at all. You see, nobody at the studio expected me to amount to anything, so when I said I would rather not have any publicity they took me at my word. Then after I had left town for a summer holiday the press began to clamour for material, and not having any facts to hand the studio obligingly made some up.'

From now on, things were going to be very different. Whether she liked it or not, and she patently didn't, Hollywood was now to be Hepburn's principal place of work and she would have to get used to its eccentric ways. Cukor was the first to try and teach her local customs: she came to see him one afternoon wearing her habitual trousers, but proudly announcing that she was on her way home from an invitation to lunch at the still-glamorous Pickfair, home of Hollywood's reigning royalty Doug Fairbanks and Mary Pickford. 'You arrived, I trust' enquired Cukor, 'through the servant's entrance?'

Hepburn retaliated by disguising herself as a parlour maid from a staff agency and serving a three-course dinner to Mrs Walter Wanger who was finally able to point out to her guests the remarkable resemblance of the maid 'to that new girl in pictures'. There was, recalled Cukor, 'a gruff, mannish quality about her which seemed to surprise and confuse people. She often looked as though she would rather be some place else.'

Her conviction that Hollywood was a curiously ill-run place was deepened by her experience on returning there from the summer in Europe. Selznick had told her that she would be starting work on *Three Came Unarmed*, a bestselling novel by E. Arnot Robertson about the daughter of an alcoholic Borneo missionary who is sent to live in Wales where her wild jungle ways shock the local residents. Kate saw herself in animal skins, carrying a spear throughout, and was much looking forward to the experience. Told, for publicity purposes, to meet her new co-star at Pasadena station, she strode womanfully down the platform and straight past a somewhat embarrassed Joel McCrea who then had rather sheepishly to give her his name. 'And what do you do?' Hepburn enquired, only to have McCrea explain that he was the star she had come to meet. They got on better when he agreed to teach her to surf, but after a few days' shooting the film was abandoned by RKO as unworkable and Hepburn was kept hanging around her small Hollywood house until the studio could come up with something else for her to do.

What they eventually found was yet another British novel, *Christopher Strong* by Gilbert Frankau, the story of a female aviator who falls in love with a married man, becomes pregnant by him and ultimately commits suicide by pulling off her oxygen mask at thirty thousand feet while going for the world altitude record – successfully, if posthumously. Hepburn was clearly now card-indexed for 'strong drama with an English background'. Her (to Californians) strange-sounding nasal voice and aristocratic appearance marked her down as somehow unAmerican in the Hollywood sense; on the other hand, she patently wasn't Scandinavian like Garbo, or German like

McCrea, an early brief Hollywood counter: 'and what do do for a living?'

Dietrich, so that left England as a natural home for her unorthodox talents. Just as thousands of his fellow-countrymen began to believe that Douglas Fairbanks Junior must have been English because of his devotion to the country, so many Americans began now to assume that Hepburn had probably come from somewhere around there too.

She had not, however, been even RKO's first choice for *Christopher Strong*. It was only when Ann Harding became unavailable, and Hepburn was all too available because of the collapse of *Three Came Unarmed*, that the film was turned over to her and then amid the loud protests of its director, another rare strong-headed female film-maker of the time called Dorothy Arzner. The sad thing is that if Hepburn had been Arzner's first choice, if she had not been thrust upon her as shooting was about to start, the two women might have got along very well indeed. As it was, there proved no time for the

creation of any sort of personal relationship: they addressed each other as 'Miss Hepburn' and 'Miss Arzner' throughout the filming, and Arzner disliked the way that Hepburn would always be speaking up for the 'little people' on the set against her often autocratic and very demanding way of working. She also had certain doubt about Hepburn as a screen actress. 'Her tone was all wrong: I had to soften her constantly . . . but sometimes she could be wonderful. There was a scene in a boat on a lake with her married lover [Colin Clive, who had come out from England with *Journey's End*] and I decided it had to be two people looking just dead ahead, two people who couldn't express any emotion – just monotonous emptiness. At first she played the scene headlong, but when I told her to look blank she did and her voice went wonderfully flat and toneless. People said it was the best love story on the screen.'

Some people did. Regina Crewe, for instance, writing of Hepburn's performance for the *Journal American*: 'That troubled, mask-like face, that high, strident, raucous, rasping voice, that straight broad-shouldered boyish figure – they may all grate on you, but they compel attention and they fascinate an audience. She is a distinct, definite, positive personality – the first since Garbo.'

Others were not so sure: *Christopher Strong* was generally reckoned to be a massive disappointment after Hepburn's initial success in *Bill of Divorcement*, and the early reviews were indeed so bad that Miss Arzner immediately abandoned her commission to work on the next Hepburn picture.

The problem with *Christopher Strong* seems to have been that, though loosely based on the Amy Johnson story, its dialogue was so ludicrously clenched ('This is pure folly') and its attitudes so frozen behind the stiff upper lips of its characters that nobody much cared what happened to them in life or death or love.

Later critics have found something fascinating in the pairing of two early Hollywood feminists on a picture as male-dominated as the industry in which they worked, but the film itself won't stand much closer examination than its heroine's motto ('Courage Conquers Death') though on first release it was left to another woman, again Regina Crewe, to leap most defiantly to Hepburn's defence. 'It cannot be denied that Katharine Hepburn, the new Hollywood glamour star, has spindly, spidery legs, a voice that at times closely resembles a klaxon with tonsilitis and hollow, starved-looking cheeks. But do these things militate against her? Far from it. Because of

'In her second film, *Christopher Strong*, Hepburn fascinates b her strange beauty a inescapable magnetis by her verve, her harshness and her tenderness. She has t enormous advantage making her every mo reflect a mental state utter sincerity and conviction.' *Los Ang Times*

'There is something finely natural about the acting of both Miss Hepburn and Colin Clive here . . . Miss Hepburn is thorough and believable and sometimes fascinatingly beautiful whether wearing aeronautical leggings, a white evening dress or a costume which (she says) makes her look like a moth. A slim, gaunt-featured nymph with a penchant for the bizarre in outfits, there is a vitality and special kind of personality here. Miss Hepburn has now definitely arrived.' *Time*

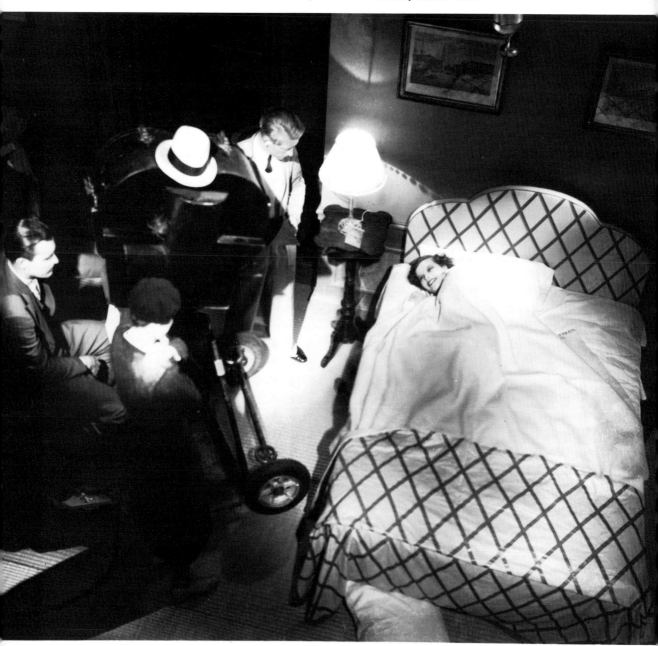

them, she will be discussed and argued about a hundred times more than if she were merely beautiful in a straightforward bathing-cutie manner. She is in fact just one more proof of the fact that it is more difficult for a really beautiful woman to become a great film personality than for a rich producer to pronounce and define "montage". Apart altogether from her physical attributes, she gives a performance in *Christopher Strong* which leaves no doubt that we have a new addition to the gallery of talkie great ones.'

Less than a year after her first arrival on the screen, London and New York audiences were lining up behind Hepburn in a way that Hollywood could never really understand: an industry which based its notions of success upon likely box-office appeal in middle America had already been invaded by a lady whose support was to come from a lot further East. Even so, nothing could save *Christopher Strong* from those who were understandably inclined to roll around in their cinema seats at lines like 'Is this goodbye, then, Harry?' and 'What a brick you are, Cynthia' and 'I died a thousand times these last two weeks' and

'Monica didn't come home at all last night', and some early support for Hepburn was visibly waning: 'Those of us who cheered her along during her marvelous performance in *A Bill of Divorcement*' noted the *World-Telegram* 'are left aghast at the amateurish quality of her histrionics. For the first half of the film she shrieks her lines in an unduly affected voice and for the rest of the time her diction is so raspish it jars on the nerves.'

She never worked with Arzner again; the end of the filming had not been helped by a severe bout of Hepburn influenza, and its generally cool critical reception did not do anything to warm Kate's still chilly feelings about Hollywood life. Forced at around this time to call a press conference to deny studio-inspired rumours that she was really the daughter of the President of the Chase Manhattan Bank (a gentleman who also happened to be called Hepburn), she then found herself fielding further questions. Asked if she had ever been married to Ogden Ludlow, and if so whether she still was (in fact yes), Hepburn stiffly replied 'I really cannot remember.' Asked whether she had any children, she answered 'Two white and three colored.'

Jokes like that, in so far as they were even recognised as jokes, were not much appreciated by a press corps more accustomed to dealing with the gracious vapidity of Mary Pickford or the efficient publicity-machine that was Joan Crawford. Garbo had already patented the 'I wish to be alone' routine, so that left Hepburn somewhere out there on her own as usual. Still, she had achieved some sort of sexual breakthrough with *Christopher Strong*: made only months before the Hays Code cracked down on Hollywood morality, it contained what Pauline Kael was to call 'the intelligent woman's primal post-coital scene'. Brendan Gill was less certain: 'early Hepburn heroines' he noted, 'gave the impression that they would make love only after marriage and then only with a certain fastidious reluctance, nostrils flaring.'

*'I came along at a point
in the movie industry when
nothing like me had ever
existed – with a loud voice
and a very definite
personality and a rather
belligerent look'*

5

HEPBURN HAD ONLY BEEN IN HOLLYWOOD SIX months, and she already had a hit and a flop under her belt: within another six months she was to to make two more hits, so that her first year did not leave a lot of time for a non-studio life. Which was maybe just as well, considering that her only real friend in California was still the one she had brought out from New York, the socialite Laura Harding. Both the men who had expressed such interest in her at first, George Cukor and David Selznick, had now moved on to other movies for other studios, leaving Hepburn to make out as best she could. Years later she recalled in conversation with David Robinson: 'I became a star before I knew how to be a star, and then I thought, well, maybe I'd better learn how to do it. The first thing to learn is that nobody must ever know how terrified you are. You've got to be very cool, even though you may be dying inside. Then, I think that we all come to town from the village with a certain amount of goodies but they don't last forever. So when you first arrive there everybody fights to buy them, and you have to learn to be a little bit cagey about who you sell them to and how many you let go.

'I was very lucky to get four big films in my first year, but whenever possible I always went back East to my family, to the place where I'd lived when I was one, two, three and so on. And I know that's where I began and where I'll be buried: most actors go away from their roots and it always shows in their performances. I stayed with the roots, and when I first got to Hollywood I stayed with RKO because it was a small studio and I knew everybody there. They were a good group, and there's a lot to be said for knowing everybody you're working with because it is so terribly embarrassing to have to keep explaining your eccentricities to strangers, to have to keep saying "I must tell you why I'm so horrible. I'm not really this way: it's just the work that pushes me." A lot of my early pictures were made in four weeks, and working like that, six days at a time from 9.30

to 5.30, I was forced to capsule my thinking and to find a kind of intensity that ruled out eating or making phone calls or doing anything other than just getting up in front of the cameras and acting.'

And suitably enough, the film with which Hepburn followed *Christopher Strong* was about just that, the obsessive life of an actress: the writer was again Zoe Akins who had done the script of *Christopher Strong*, only this time what she had come up with (originally as an unproduced play) was the classic tale of the small-town girl who goes out there and comes back a star. Essentially *Morning Glory* was *42nd Street* without the songs, and it was indeed the film in which Adolphe Menjou got to say to Hepburn, after her triumphal arrival at stardom, 'You don't belong to any man now, you belong to Broadway!'

But though she was to get the first of her four Oscars for it, *Morning Glory* did not originally belong to Hepburn at all: loosely based on the story of Tallulah Bankhead, it had been intended as a vehicle for another RKO contract star, Constance Bennett, and Bankhead herself was not pleased to have lost the role in her own early story to 'that prude Hepburn'. Years later, when the women had become firm friends, Bankhead was to revise her opinion: 'Whenever I go to see a Hepburn film I start by wondering why on earth she speaks like that, and by the end of the film I wonder why everybody doesn't.'

The scripting of *Morning Glory* was badly affected by the sudden death of Zoe Akins's husband, and the finished film (which also bears a writing credit for Howard J. Green) leaves few backstage clichés unturned. The director, Lowell Sherman, was John Barrymore's brother-in-law and had himself been the star of Cukor's *What Price Hollywood* before alcoholism forced him to move behind the camera, and the whole movie was saturated by molten greasepaint. As it opens, Hepburn is walking through a theatre foyer hung with the

A star is born: Hepburn as the actress (and Douglas Fairbanks Jr as the actor) in RKO's 1933 *Morning Glory*: 'You don't belong to any man now—you belong to Broadway.' *Adolphe Menjou.*

photographs of Ethel Barrymore, Sarah Bern-
hardt and Maude Adams on her way to see
Menjou. Soon, Ada Love of Franklin Vermont
has become Eva Lovelace, and Hepburn gets
the chance to do her Ophelia and her Juliet at
breakneck speed before a convenient star
tantrum allows her to go out front while Aubrey
Smith (already the veteran counsellor) advises
her that she has to be careful of becoming 'a
morning glory – a flower that fades before the
sun is very high'.

Remade inadequately a quarter of a century
later as *Stage Struck*, with Susan Strasberg
playing Ada Love, Zoe Akins's screenplay was
in the view of most critics hopelessly artificial
and not much helped by the playing of Menjou
as the producer or Douglas Fairbanks Junior as
a lovelorn dramatist. But about Hepburn's
arrival at fully-fledged stardom there was no
doubt: the London *Times* thought that 'in a
depressingly second-rate story she admirably
mingles intellectual austerity with physical
gaucherie' while on her own home territory
even *Time* acknowledged that: 'from this
immemorial fairy tale the delicate, muscled face
of Heroine Hepburn shines out like a face on
a coin. Of the brash little provincial she makes
a strangely distinguished character, a little mad
from hunger and dreams, absurdly audacious
and trusting. Since *Christopher Strong* she has
toned down her strident voice, taken off some
of her angular swank in gesture and strut, found
other ways to register emotion than by dilating
her nostrils.'

Reviews like that one made Kate a certainty
for her first Oscar nomination: the competition
was not too strong (Diana Wynyard for
Cavalcade, May Robson for *Lady For A Day*)
and though *Morning Glory* showed up nowhere
else in the year's honours it did get Hepburn the
first of her four statues with little difficulty. Hollywood had always loved the story of a little girl
from nowhere becoming a star, as three
remakes of *A Star is Born* were later to prove.

'As an antidote to the febrile dramas of the underworld and backstage musical spectacles, *Little Women* comes as a reminder that emotions and vitality and truth can be evoked from lavender and lace as well as from machine guns and precision dances . . . It is a tribute to those who shared in bringing it to the screen that there is no betrayal here, either of the spirit or of the feeling of the original. The hoydenish Jo is capitally performed by Katharine Hepburn; Joan Bennett is excellent as Amy, as are Frances Dee and Jean Parker as Meg and Beth. Also, director George Cukor and the producers deserve praise for a production that has been carried out with taste as well as skill *New York Post*.
Below, Hepburn with Douglass Montgomery and George Cukor.

Hepburn herself had been honoured by the Academy for playing on screen precisely the kind of nowhere girl she had resolutely refused to be off-screen, and feelings between her and the studios were still somewhat strained after the award. As one gossip columnist of the time indignantly noted: 'A skinny, freckled, snooty typhoon Kate has hit Hollywood: she immediately set out to break all the rules and was as unpleasant and unco-operative as possible. She fought senselessly with practically everyone from top producers to lowest technicians. She was insulting and abusive to the press and gave out ridiculous and inane interviews in which she deliberately distorted the facts of her personal life. She allowed herself to be photographed without make-up, in all her freckles, and even worse she dressed hideously in a mannish garb – sloppy slacks, sweaters and men's trousers and suits. She hired a Rolls Royce to take her to the studio and she read her fan mail sitting on the curb outside the RKO lot.'

In truth it seems unlikely that Hepburn bothered deliberately to annoy the Hollywood establishment, and those who like Cukor and Selznick took the trouble to get to know her always reported favourably: she did however have a lot to learn about the techniques of being an actress, and saw no reason why she should overload an already crowded work schedule with the time it would take to learn the techniques of being a film star. Nevertheless, some people were determined to dub her 'Katharine of Arrogance' while others rapidly became obsessed by her precisely because she was both physically and emotionally so unlike any other actress working in Hollywood in the early thirties. One of her very first suitors out there was the ever-romantic Doug Fairbanks Junior who had been with her in *Morning Glory* and spent three months trying to persuade her to have dinner with him. When, long after the film was finished, she finally consented he was hurt to discover her pleading a sick headache halfway through the meal and still more hurt when,

having returned her home, he noticed her immediately leave the house with a quite different suitor.

This was almost certainly her agent Leland Hayward, with whom she had started an affair which was to be the most important of her life until the meeting with Spencer Tracy. Hayward was an elegant and unusually cultured Hollywood fixer much given to living with (and occasionally marrying) his clients, a starry bunch who ranged from Hepburn through Margaret Sullavan to Ginger Rogers and Miriam Hopkins. It was Hayward who, more than anyone since her father, gave Hepburn a kind of style and a kind of courage with which to mask the terror she still felt at going before the cameras, he who understood that she was a thoroughbred who could stay the course if properly handled. And he who managed, after *Morning Glory*, to get her back with the two film-makers who really understood her, Selznick and Cukor.

By this time, early in 1933, they had started to work on a screen version of *Little Women*,

Katharine Hepburn

the Louisa May Alcott tale of four girls growing up into womanhood while their father is away at the Civil War. Selznick was now leaving RKO for MGM, so Cukor was left to convince the studio that their first two draft screenplays would have to be abandoned, as would all attempts to modernise the story. Instead, he recommended that they go all out for accurate period detail. Cukor had always managed to avoid reading the book (Hepburn was later to accuse him of never having finished it even during the shooting) but when Selznick did finally urge it on him he found to his relief that reports of a saccharine-sweet sentimentality were misleading. 'It's full of an admirable New England kind of sternness and survival, and Kate Hepburn casts something very special over it coming from that same large family background. Like Garbo and *Camille*, she was born to play Jo. She's tender and funny, fiercely loyal, and plays the fool when she feels like it. There's a purity about her. Kate and Jo are the same girl: you could go with whatever she did on the set, though I always used many weapons in dealing with her – simulated rage, ridicule, good-humoured cajolery.'

Hepburn achieved solo star billing for the first time with *Little Women*, and in return she gave Jo a remarkable kind of angular, athletic, slangy, tomboyish accuracy. But with the completion of that film, her fourth in twelve months, her thoughts began to turn back towards the New York theatre she had never really conquered. The producer Jed Harris, then Broadway's boy wonder with a string of recent hits from *The Front Page* back to *Broadway* itself, had bought an English play called *The Lake* by Dorothy Massingham and Murray Macdonald, and thought he might be able to tempt Hepburn back to Broadway with it. He had actually first tried to get her for *The Green Bay Tree* which he was staging with Olivier, but Hepburn thought the female role in that too minor considering the movie stardom she had recently achieved, so it went instead to the actress she had beaten a year earlier to *Bill of Divorcement*, Jill Esmond. Now Harris was trying again, though his opinion of Hepburn was never of the highest: 'she didn't have brains or anything like that,' he later wrote, 'she was just a terribly stage-struck girl with certain odd components which I thought would be successful in the theatre.'

Accordingly he sent her *The Lake*, the clenched tale of an English girl called Stella Surrege whose husband drowns on the way from the wedding reception to the honeymoon, thereby allowing her to reshape her life in a more suitable direction. Harris himself thought it was 'common, stupid and sentimental' but Hepburn's eagerness to play it for him in New York convinced him 'for the only time in my whole life in the theatre to venture into "show business" which is all that *The Lake* with Hepburn amounted to.'

First, however, there was the matter of her RKO contract: the studio agreed to release her for the time it would take to do *The Lake* on Broadway provided she first make one more film for them, and do it in a month for fifty thousand dollars. The film they had in mind was

KATHARINE
HEPBURN
Spitfire

WITH
ROBERT YOUNG
RALPH BELLAMY
MARTHA SLEEPER
FROM THE PLAY BY LULA VOLLMER
DIRECTED BY JOHN CROMWELL
A PANDRO S. BERMAN MERIAN C. COOPER
PRODUCTION EXECUTIVE PRODUCER

RKO
Radio
PICTURES

Spitfire, a remarkably daft piece for which she was cast as a young tomboy faith-healer who comes down from the Ozark mountains to kidnap a neglected baby and falls in love with a friendly neighbourhood engineer (Ralph Bellamy). This was not, to put it mildly, a success: 'Miss Hepburn's Southern accent' thought the *New York Post* 'is pitched somewhere between Amos and Andy and is no more convincing than either', while even the usually enthusiastic *New Yorker* had to admit that Kate was less than ideally cast as 'a sad little thing much given to prayer and savage rows with her neighbours'.

Years later, Ken Tynan was to call Hepburn 'the Garbo of the Great Outdoors' but this first venture into the open air suggested that she still had a lot to learn. One or two critics tried to be charitable however, and the *New Statesman* thought that 'despite one of the most tedious stories ever told on the screen, and rather too many shots of Miss Hepburn praying with a convenient back-light diffused through her hair, her obvious conviction that she is an actress may have some reasonable basis in fact.'

Shaking the dust of the Ozarks off her RKO contract, Hepburn then headed for Broadway, only to find that things were not a lot better there. Having decided to sell out his artistic soul by putting on a movie star in a supposedly popular vehicle, Harris proceeded to vent his wrath on the movie star herself all through rehearsals. Almost fifty years later, in a rare inteview granted for five hundred dollars to Charles Higham, Mr Harris was still vitriolic about Hepburn: 'I could see she was hopeless. I fought with her – I begged her to stop posing, striking attitudes, leaning against doorways, putting a limp hand to her forehead, to stop being a big movie star and feel the lines, feel the character. I was trying the impossible, to make an artificial showcase for an artificial star, and she couldn't handle it ... it was as though she had seen her own performance, like her own rather charming babbling at everything, and decided that was acting.'

'Miss Hepburn is so young, unsophisticated, idealistic: so very, very J. M. Barrie. She always makes her young women quite horrifyingly lifelike with their girlish intuitions, their intensity and their ideals which destroy the edge of human pleasure.' *Graham Greene*, 1935

Back to Broadway with Colin Clive in *The Lake* **(1933):**
'The simple fact is that as a result of her sensational
achievements on the screen she has been projected into a
stage part that requires more versatility than she has
had time to develop. She still needs considerable
training, especially for a voice that has an unpleasant
timbre.' *New York Times*.
'She is not a great actress, certainly, but she has a
certain distinction which might with training possibly
take the place of great acting in an emergency.'
Robert Benchley

In all fairness it should be added that Harris
already had a reputation as one of the most
savage and anti-actor directors in town, and
that this may well have been a power struggle
in which he found that for once the actress had
rather too many of the aces: films were still new
enough in those days for remarkably few of
their stars to have returned to Broadway, while
local New York talent tended to be more sub-
missive because it had not yet discovered any
other place of employment. Rehearsals went
from bad to worse, Hepburn quarrelled even
with such fellow-players as Colin Clive who had
been with her in *Christopher Strong*, and by the
time they got to Washington, Harris was all for
abandoning the entire venture. Here however
he ran into another new problem: because of
Hepburn's sudden screen stardom (*Spitfire* had
mercifully not yet been released) the New York
theatre which had announced *The Lake* as a

forthcoming attraction had already taken forty
thousand dollars in advance booking on the
strength of her name alone. There was thus to
be no question of a quiet closure in
Washington.

Looking back on the whole unhappy production, Harris conceded that 'I should have been
more patient with her, more considerate. I
should have paid more attention to her. I felt
sorry for her – she had spent her whole so-called
love life with a nonentity she married called
Smith, and then she was involved with an agent,
for God's sake, called Leland Hayward. She
was an imbecile, a damn fool, an idiot, yet I
regret I wasn't more patient – there was a bar-
rier of language and feeling I could not cross to
reach her.'

So *The Lake* struggled on into New York,
where it opened on the day after Christmas 1933
and did at least make one great reputation. Not

'There is little doubt that the star of *The Little Minister* is one of the major wonder workers of Hollywood. Miss Hepburn has an unconquerable gift for turning lavender and old lace into something possessing dramatic vitality and conviction . . . she provides this film with much of the charm that went into the miracle of *Little Women*.'
New York Herald Tribune

Hepburn's, not Harris's, nor anyone actually involved with the production, but a critic called Dorothy Parker who in the course of an otherwise unremarkable review of the first night achieved immortality with one line: 'Miss Hepburn' she wrote, 'ran the gamut of emotions from A to B.'

Other critics were kinder, but not a lot, and one of the severest was Hepburn herself: 'On opening night I was simply petrified. My voice went all loony and I must have been as stiff as a board. I'm sure my performance was foul.' Professional reviewers generally concurred; the actress whom a year or two earlier they had been prepared to acclaim as at least 'promising' had now, they gleefully proclaimed, been 'ruined' by Hollywood techniques. If there was one thing Broadway critics hated more than a Hollywood movie star, it was a Hollywood movie star who had deserted the legitimate theatre in New York for what they saw as nothing better than a seaside resort offering sunshine, oranges and instant fame, as well as a lot more money than could be made back East. Intriguingly another movie star on her way back to Broadway at this time (and one bearing many similarities to Hepburn in pioneering feminine courage) was Lillian Gish: she however had been formally rejected by movies after the coming of sound, and was therefore welcomed back to Broadway by critics who rightly wanted to point out the lunacy of a California where an actress of that calibre could be cast out. With Hepburn there was the firm suspicion that she was not back on Broadway to stay, but only to test out her new-found fame in front of a live audience. And on those terms precious few were prepared to give her the benefit of the doubt on a first night which she herself admitted was catastrophic.

There remained the problem of those forty thousand dollars already taken at the box-office: reviews were by no means bad enough to deter people who had already bought tickets in advance, and a good many other theatre-goers were sufficiently intrigued by them to want to go along and see if Hepburn was really as bad as the papers had made out. In fact, by the time they got there, she wasn't: once the first-night nerves were over and Mr Harris had stopped browbeating her at rehearsal, Hepburn calmly learnt how to play the part and by all later accounts played it very well indeed. But she had been depressed by the initial reaction, ('Miss Hepburn' wrote George Jean Nathan, dean of the Broadway critics, 'has many of the qualities that may one day make her an actress of position . . . but that day is still far from being at hand') and it had killed any affection she'd once had for *The Lake*. Now she wanted out.

In fact, Harris had never bothered to give her a formal contract, but they had an unwritten agreement that Kate would do six months on Broadway, and Hepburn was not one to break even a verbal undertaking of that kind. Five weeks into the run (by which time most of the advance had been used up) she approached Harris and asked him what it would cost to buy

herself out of the show. Harris estimated fifteen thousand dollars, which was not a lot to Hepburn considering that she'd managed to get ten thousand out of RKO for just one day's overtime on *Spitfire*. Accordingly she paid up, and *The Lake* closed on 10 February 1934. Two days later she sailed for Europe, having that morning heard the good news of her Oscar win for *Morning Glory*.

After a brisk European vacation, a brief return to New York to sign the lease on an East 49th St brownstone house she had discovered during the run of *The Lake* and where she lives to this day, and an even more brief visit to Yucatan in Mexico to formalise the divorce from Ogden Ludlow, Hepburn reported back for work in Hollywood early in the summer of 1934. RKO, keen to capitalise on her success in *Little Women*, offered her another period piece in J. M. Barrie's *The Little Minister* which Hepburn was distinctly unenthusiastic about until she heard that it was also on offer to Margaret Sullavan, already her rival for the affections of their mutual agent Leland Hayward. At once, Kate accepted: 'several of the roles I played in those early years' she later admitted with disarming candour, 'were ones that I only wanted after I heard that another actress really needed them.'

Barrie's twee tale of a Scots aristocrat disguising herself as a gypsy and falling for the local preacher had already been filmed twice as a silent, and on stage it had been a favourite role of Maude Adams, the actress many thought Hepburn most resembled and whom she had always admired. There was however something desperately uneasy about the Laurel Canyon recreation of 1840s Scotland, and in the title role John Beal could most charitably be described as wooden. But RKO, encouraged by the success of *Little Women* and convinced that (with the arrival of the Hays Code and a new puritanism) their best hope lay in schoolroom 'classics', put an unprecedented six hundred and fifty thousand dollars into the budget, mak-

A 1934 screen test for a sadly unmade *Saint Joan*: 'How long, Oh Lord, how long before the earth will be ready to receive thy Saints?' Ingrid Bergman and Jean Seberg both went to the stake in later film versions, but Hepburn's would have been the one to watch.

ing it far and away the most expensive picture in which Hepburn had ever appeared. Nor were they inclined to undersell what they were sure was going to be the Christmas hit at Radio City in New York: Hepburn was billed on the posters simply by her surname in huge block capitals above the legend 'More thrilling . . . More disturbing . . . More fascinating than Ever' and in case that message was regarded as too subtle, they added 'Only the greatest actress of her time could have breathed life into the most magnetic heroine of all time.'

Critics reported an overpowering smell of lavender and old lace, but though they were respectful enough ('Hepburn is one of the major wonder-workers of Hollywood' noted Richard Watts), a Depression audience stayed away in its thousands, preferring the musical escapism that RKO were then also offering with Fred Astaire and Ginger Rogers to the worthy piety of Barrie's period romance. *The Little Minister*

lost nearly ten thousand dollars, and following hard on the failure of the awful *Spitfire* it caused Pandro S. Berman (then head of RKO production) an agonised reappraisal of his Hepburn contract. True, she was still the Oscar-winning actress of *Morning Glory*, and she had given the studio a trio of other hits with *Little Women*, *Bill of Divorcement* and *Christopher Strong*. But now she'd had two flops in a row, one of them a costly prestige job, and Berman was suddenly appalled. 'I realised that Kate wasn't a movie star. She wasn't going to become a star either, at least not in the sense that Crawford or Shearer were actresses able to drag an audience in by their own efforts. She was a hit only in hit pictures: she couldn't save a flop. And she almost invariably chose the wrong vehicles.'

That verdict, delivered early in 1935 when Hepburn had made five films in less than three years, was the one that was to condition the rest of her Hollywood career.

61

'I strike people as peculiar
in some way, although
I don't quite understand
why; of course, I have
an angular face, an
angular body, and I suppose,
an angular personality
which jabs into people.'

6

RKO WERE NOW IN A STATE OF SUPPRESSED panic about what they were to do with the actress who was supposed to be one of their most valuable contract properties. Various possibilities were suggested, including a *Saint Joan* and a *Queen Elizabeth* (this in a script unpromisingly entitled *Tudor Wench*), as well as a life of Nell Gwynn. When none of those worked out, Kate considered a return to the stage (summer stock, rather than Broadway) either in *Dark Victory* or else in *Pride and Prejudice*. That didn't happen either, however, and all too soon she found herself back in front of the cameras. RKO decided that after the flop of *Little Minister*, costume dramas were out and cast her for a remarkably maudlin soap opera called *Break of Hearts*, about a budding composer (Hepburn) who falls in love with a distinguished conductor (Charles Boyer) and manages to save him at the last from the demon drink by joining him at the piano for their favourite song (Boyer's role was first intended for John Barrymore, at least until he read the script, and then for Francis Lederer but he was sacked at Hepburn's instigation after a week of shooting.) 'There is probably nobody in pictures today who needs a money film as much as Hepburn does now' noted an acute observer, but sadly *Break of Hearts* was certainly not it. 'Mae West and Mickey Mouse' added one English critic, 'are the only two current Hollywood stars who have not recently appeared in a version of the plot which now concerns Hepburn and Boyer. In Hepburn RKO have one of the greatest screen stars in the world: what a pity they have not the remotest idea of what to do with her.'

Away from the studios, Hepburn's life was not working out any better than her career. The affair with Hayward was almost over, the dream of triumphant return to her stage home in New York had been drowned in *The Lake*, and she was now in a California climate she never much cared for, surrounded by movie people with whom she had little in common,

and wishing she were back home in Hartford with her beloved and ever-loving family. To have gone, however, would have been to admit a kind of defeat, and she was never a lady to do that: instead she decided long before most of her studio-contracted contemporaries that if she was ever to work in good scripts with good directors, she had better go out and find them herself. So she went out and found Booth Tarkington's *Seventeen* and William Wyler to direct it. RKO were having none of that, however, and put her instead into another and lesser-known Tarkington novel called *Alice Adams* about a small-town girl pretending to be wealthy in order to catch a husband.

Instead of Wyler they gave her George Stevens as director, and some indication of Hepburn's current standing at RKO may be gleaned from the fact that Stevens had thus far worked mainly in two-reel comedies with Wheeler and Woolsey. Fred MacMurray, another newcomer to first features, was cast as the young man, with Hattie McDaniel as a scene-stealing black maid, and *Alice Adams* had all the makings of a low-budget programme filler.

But then something very curious happened: despite a difficult time on the set, where neither Hepburn nor Stevens seemed to have much faith in the other, and despite initially gloomy reports, *Alice Adams* turned out to be a sizeable hit and one which won for Hepburn her second Oscar nomination, though on the night she lost out to Bette Davis.

The film seemed to catch a small-town American nostalgia, and the critic on *Time* now thought that: 'Though Katharine Hepburn is possibly the least versatile of all Hollywood's leading stars, it is precisely this limitation which makes her ideal for *Alice*. The woebegone grimaces, the expressions half-childish and half-addleheaded so startlingly misplaced in her portrayals of women of the world, are precisely those which make her portrayal of a girl she really understands her masterpiece to date.'

As the glamorous Constance Dane in *Break of Hearts*, left; and in more homely guise as *Alice Adams* (also 1935) with co-star Fred MacMurray and director George Stevens: 'What was in 1922 a shrewd and observant novel emerges now as a bitingly satiric portrait of an era . . . Katharine Hepburn has never looked more stunning, nor played with such distinction, authority or charm.' *Time*

With Cary Grant, Edmund Gwenn, Brian Aherne and director George Cukor in the baroque transvestite Compton Mackenzie folly that was *Sylvia Scarlett* (1936) and overleaf: 'The dynamic Miss Hepburn is the handsomest boy of the season. I am forced to say that her vehicle is a sprawling and ineffective essay in dramatic chaos, with characters and situations enmeshed in vague obscurities, but for Miss Hepburn's performance in the title role I have nothing but admiration.' *Richard Watts*

Stevens remained unconvinced ('she not only has no technique' he told a colleague after the shooting, 'she seems to want none') but audiences all over America were now willing to take Hepburn back to their hearts, safely wrapped in the 1922 charm of a Tarkington tale that many believed had been responsible for his Pulitzer Prize.

And RKO were duly grateful: indeed Berman, in what he would later see as an excess of enthusiasm, told Hepburn that because of her triumphant *Alice* – which took ninety thousand dollars in its first week at the Radio City where she was billed as 'America's Greatest Actress' – she really could choose her next film and its director. Not surprisingly, she went straight back to Cukor, her lifelong favourite and about the only man in Hollywood apart from Hayward whose company she could bear on a personal as well as professional level. And Cukor had an idea. He had been reading, with considerable delight, a 1918 novel by Compton Mackenzie called *The Early Adventures of Sylvia Scarlett* which was a sort of updated *As You Like It*, largely concerned with a tacit kind of bisexuality. An initial critical and box-office disaster that has now become a collectors' piece for Cukor, Hepburn and Cary Grant addicts the world over, *Sylvia Scarlett* told the story of a trio of confidence tricksters: Sylvia herself (Hepburn), her father (Edmund Gwenn) and a cockney adventurer (Grant) they collect along the way. To escape detection after an earlier escapade in France, Sylvia has disguised herself as a man: then however she begins to fall in love, first with Cary Grant and later with Brian Aherne, and has to choose not only between them but also whether to carry on living as a man or as a woman.

It's not difficult to see what attracted the ever-anglophile Cukor and Kate (who was later on stage to play both Shakespeare's leading transvestites in *As You Like It* and *Twelfth Night*) to this whimsical, fey, ambiguous but often enchanting piece. What is harder to

fathom is why RKO allowed Hepburn even to start thinking of appearing in a film which would disguise her as a man throughout, and why Paramount, having refused to loan Cary Grant out to MGM for the prestigious *Mutiny on the Bounty*, cheerfully let him go instead to RKO for these distinctly dubious proceedings. Even Hepburn seems to have had her doubts in mid-shoot: 'A lot of pictures of mine that people thought bad at the time have since been called "classics", but of those *Sylvia Scarlett* is the most surprising. I remember going home one night from the studio and writing in my diary "This picture makes no sense at all and I wonder whether George Cukor is aware of the fact, because I certainly don't know what the hell I'm doing".'

And if Hepburn, most unusually for her, had not the faintest idea what she was doing then neither did anybody else except possibly Cukor, and even he decided at the last minute to shoot a whole prologue showing Hepburn with long flowing hair and dresses, presumably in case audiences thought she really was a boy: as Brian Aherne says when he first starts to fall in love with her as a man, 'there's something very queer going on here'. But it was not something Californian audiences of 1935 either understood or cared for: Kate recalled a horrendous preview at which the customers fairly rushed for the doors when she started on screen to recite a poem by Edna St Vincent Millay: 'Then when the final credits had rolled to stunned silence, I went to the ladies' room and a woman was lying on the floor with her eyes raised to heaven and I said jovially "Are you overcome by our picture?" and she just closed her eyes and did not even answer me. Then I got into George's car which had a very low roof and hit my head and thought maybe I'd luckily been knocked unconscious, but I hadn't so we drove back to meet Pandro Berman, the producer and I – always eager to fix everything up – said well, not to worry, George and I would just agree to do another film for him for nothing to make up for

this disaster. And Berman went sort of green and said it wasn't a question of money, he just never wanted to make another picture with either of us as long as we lived.'

A number of other people had already had lucky escapes from *Sylvia Scarlett*. Cukor had offered the screenplay to Evelyn Waugh and one of the minor roles to Mrs Patrick Campbell, both of whom turned it down, but the film did in fact establish Cary Grant for the first time as an actor rather than just a charm merchant, and though he was only getting fifteen thousand dollars to Hepburn's fifty, it established a starring partnership between them which was to carry over into three big successes in the years immediately ahead.

But for now, *Sylvia Scarlett* was a real problem: what Cukor and Hepburn had thought of as a quirky little black comedy had achieved the dimensions of a scandalous romp about criminals of dubious sexuality, and one moreover which was to lose RKO over three hundred and sixty thousand dollars in its first year of release. *Time* magazine thought its only claim to fame was in 'revealing the interesting fact that Katharine Hepburn is better looking as a boy than as a woman', and the *New York Times* critic could only bring himself to record the time the film started and how long it lasted. Set in a never-never recreation of rural England ('We achieved Picaresque right here in Laurel Canyon' noted Cukor; 'the White Cliffs of Dover were just beyond Malibu, the same place we used for *David Copperfield*') and played by Hepburn, Grant, Aherne and Gwenn as if they were a company of strolling tumblers, *Sylvia Scarlett* was said to have been inspired by the arrest of Dr Crippen's mistress disguised as a boy but in fact owed its loyalties as a film to a vastly more confused background of English fairy-tale fantasy. At one moment in the film, when Hepburn is about to leave Grant for Aherne, Cary warns her 'I give you one word of advice – don't try to step out of your class' and it serves as an epitaph for a film which tried

to step way outside all boundaries of studio behaviour and was accordingly punished by the critics and audiences alike.

Predictably, the English liked it a lot more than the Americans, and the New Yorkers liked it more than the Californians; Hepburn's power-base in the cinema always strengthened the further East her films travelled, but the roguish whimsy of this one strained even the loyalists. It was one of those rare and fatal pictures in which everyone seems to have been having a wonderful time except the audience, and for Berman it was quite simply 'the worst picture by far that I ever made, and the greatest catastrophe of Kate's career. She and Cukor conned me into it, claiming it was the greatest thing they had ever found. I couldn't understand a thing that was going on.'

RKO now had a real problem with Hepburn, as Berman was the first to acknowledge: 'Her career was having its ups and downs. Who was to blame? Well, we were, primarily. Kate was RKO's biggest individual star. She and the team of Astaire and Rogers were the backbone of the studio. We turned out so many Hepburn pictures each season, whether they were right or wrong for her, whether scripts were ready or not ready. But we still hadn't found Kate's formula: I don't mean that she is limited or has to be typed, but that a certain character line suits her best. And that line happens to correspond to Kate's own character. She can't be namby-pamby or stickily sentimental. She has to have a certain arrogance which audiences then like to see humbled, but without breaking her spirit.'

But far and away the most considered assessment of Hepburn's problems at this time came from Alistair Cooke, making the last in a series of BBC broadcasts about the cinema before setting sail to America from where he would soon start sending his celebrated Letters: 'It seemed when Katharine Hepburn first appeared in *Morning Glory* that she had an almost painful surplus of charm, so that she could have given you and me a handful of it and still left us dull ... but she is still having to wait for her producers to do right by her. I suppose when you've been launched as a star, nothing short of high tragedy will do for you. Your emotions have to be in scale, and if I know anything about studio methods those emotions are probably plotted on a graph and rise and fall in proportion to the dollars spent on any given scene. But it seems a pity that so sharp and sensitive a person as Katharine Hepburn should have to bear the brunt of being a star. She's probably itching to show us how charming she can be when she sneezes or blows her nose but "Come, come" she hears the voice of the studio executives calling to her, "you may be Kate to your pals but you're La Hepburn to us". And so she must not feel sad or sniffle in a corner. She must wear a

'It is possible to object, and object forcibly, to the casting of Katharine Hepburn as *Mary of Scotland*. But I will not protest too strenuously against the view that Miss Hepburn has succeeded beyond expectation, and that in her vital, sincere and impressive performance she registers a new triumph. That is not my personal view, but at least I understand it. Her accent is not of the Highlands, the Lowlands or a pure French equivalent. It is pure Hepburn and nothing else.' *London Times*.

Katharine **HEPBURN**
Fredric **MARCH**
in
MARY OF SCOTLAND

WITH
FLORENCE ELDRIDGE
DOUGLAS WALTON
JOHN CARRADINE
and a Tremendous Cast
of Famous Stars

FROM THE PLAY BY
MAXWELL ANDERSON
PRODUCED BY
PANDRO S. BERMAN

DIRECTED BY **JOHN FORD**

long gown and throw back her head at an angle of ninety degrees and let us see tears that come from depths Shakespeare never knew.'

And sure enough, La Hepburn now had to be found a suitably stellar vehicle that would repair the damage of *Sylvia Scarlett*: she had to be set back on the RKO throne and how better than by playing a doomed and tragic queen? What Kate actually wanted to do at this time was Viola in *Twelfth Night*, on stage at the Hollywood Bowl for the great Max Reinhardt. RKO however still had one picture of her contract to make, and they weren't letting her go off into any more arty rubbish like Shakespeare. Instead, what they had lined up for her was a hugely respectable if catastrophically dull costume drama from the Madame Tussaud's school of history. This was Maxwell Anderson's 1933 Broadway hit *Mary of Scotland* which had proved a sturdy vehicle for Helen Hayes and was now to be reverentially transferred to the screen with Fredric March playing the Earl of Bothwell who had been, so studio publicity gleefully noted 'distantly related to the Hepburn family on her father's side'.

But not even John Ford as director (and, it was briefly rumoured, Kate's lover) was able to breathe much life into a waxwork project through which, thought *Time*, 'Miss Hepburn strides like a Bryn Mawr senior in a May Day pageant'. Miss Hepburn herself was inclined to agree: 'There I did think I was terribly bad. I liked working with Jack Ford very much: he and I were great friends. But he was as unsuited to that material as I was unsuited to *Mary of Scotland* as an actress. I can't stand Mary of Scotland. I think she was an absolute ass. I would have loved to play Elizabeth: now she was a fascinating creature. But I had no patience with Mary. I thought Elizabeth was absolutely right to have her condemned to death. Mary was extremely silly: she fascinates some people, but not me.'

A verdict with which most of the film's viewers were forced to agree: the critic on

73

Variety thought as entertainment it suffered
badly from 'shadows, chatter and length, but
the film did nonetheless restore Hepburn to the
realms of 'safe studio stardom' after the considerably more intriguing and dangerous fiasco
of *Sylvia Scarlett*, and it allowed her to nego-
tiate a new RKO contract guaranteeing her two
hundred thousand dollars for her next four
movies. The studio may still have been unsure
of what to do with her, but for as long as she
went on collecting reviews like Otis Ferguson's
they knew they could not let her go. 'For when
the spotlight and the scenic effects [on *Mary of
Scotland*] have faded, there still remains the fact
that for all her digressions into mannerism and
poor parts, for all her naïve reliance on her own
resources and befuddled trying, this girl with
the curious wide mouth and lips and flesh tight
over the facial bones is an artist by virtue of
combining personal strength and fire with the
grace of giving out to people. Her work is not
mimicry or in a ridiculous building of many
parts but it is creative in itself, a sort of bright
emanation.'

And having got her back into costume for
Mary of Scotland, RKO decided they would
leave her there for two more pictures. The first
of these was *A Woman Rebels*, a suffragette
drama set in Victorian England, shot in fifty
days and mainly notable now for having
introduced Van Heflin in a minor role: Hepburn was to be one of his most constant
champions at RKO, and later took him back to
Broadway with her for *The Philadelphia Story*.
Beyond that, the film seems to have been of
remarkably little interest even to its makers, but
RKO were so determined that Hepburn's
appeal lay in period costume pieces that they
then moved her straight into another J. M. Barrie, *Quality Street*, having apparently forgotten
the fate of *The Little Minister* only three years
earlier. Looking back on it, even Hepburn's
regular producer Pandro Berman couldn't
recall why they ever thought it would work:
'Here we were, in the middle of the Depression,

Right, with director George Stevens on the set of
Quality Street, **and below, actress turns camera operator.**

doing a story about Phoebe Throssel whose beau, Dr Valentine Brown, courts her during the Napoleonic Wars but never gets around to proposing. Jesus Christ: there are breadlines, and people are supposed to care about a rich girl in crinolines carrying a parasol and tossing up between several handsome young men? Maybe we thought it was escapist fare or some god-damned thing like that. Well, the only thing that escaped was our money – down the drain.'

Marion Davies had done a silent version of *Quality Street* a decade earlier which had worked well enough, but times, as Berman noted, were now rather different and the best that critics could see was a tired gaiety clinging to the lacy and voluminous folds of the plot. 'Miss Hepburn's Phoebe' added Frank Nugent, 'needs a neurologist far more than a husband. Such flutterings and jitterings and twitchings, such hand-wringings and mouth-quiverings, such runnings about and eyebrow-raisings have not been seen on a screen in many a moon.'

The director was again George Stevens, whom Hepburn had hauled away from a film he much wanted to make, *Winterset*, and he accordingly found it hard to forgive her: 'I don't think I did her any good: she became precious, and preciousness was always her weakness: I should have helped her away from that but I wasn't strong enough and I myself didn't have sufficient familiarity with the British background to save her. I was thinking about *Winterset* all through the shooting – my bitter disappointment at not making what could have been my best picture – and that affected me too. That's it in sum: I gave in to her, and the film was bad, and it's all my fault.'

Still, it did launch Joan Fontaine's film career, again in a very minor role but again carefully watched by Hepburn: 'At dawn, on location, Miss Hepburn would streak onto the RKO ranch in her station wagon, dressed in her habitual slacks, her auburn hair flying. At noon, wicker baskets of lunch for the cast were brought from her car. To be invited to join the picnicking group was a singular honour, and I found Hepburn as fascinating then as in some of her later plays when you felt she could have read the telephone book and I often wished she had . . . but I probably owe my motion picture career to her: she told RKO to give me the leads in some B pictures and they gave me sixteen'.

One of the many ironies of Hepburn's RKO career was that she was vastly better able to get the studio to manage other people's careers than her own. Indeed after the failure of *Quality Street*, (which coincided in her private life with the news that Leland Hayward had married Margaret Sullavan: Kate sent them a good-luck cable which Sullavan ostentatiously tore up at the reception) the studio announced with an almost audible sigh of relief that Miss Hepburn would for a while be giving up motion pictures and going back to her 'first love, the Broadway stage'.

What had happened was that on one of her many visits home to her family and New York, Hepburn had again met Lawrence Langner, Theresa Helburn and Langner's wife Armina Marshall who together ran the Theatre Guild which had once briefly employed her for *Month in the Country*. Now, in view of her controversial but undoubted RKO stardom, they were keen to put her into a Broadway production of *Jane Eyre* opposite Laurence Olivier at a thousand dollars a week. Hepburn held out successfully for fifteen hundred, on the grounds that she had been shamefully underpaid by them a decade earlier in *Month in the Country*. The Guild agreed, only then to discover that Olivier was unavailable and that no other leading actor of the time seemed exactly eager to take on Rochester opposite Kate's Jane: her track record in the theatre had not been all that wonderful, and even if *Jane Eyre* did not turn out to be another *Lake* there was still no doubt that it was likely to be a one-woman show.

Eventually however the Guild managed to come up with Dennis Hoey, an adequate if unexciting character man, and rehearsals started in the late fall of 1936; the plan was to open in New Haven, move on to Boston and then reach Broadway early in 1937. By the time they got to Boston, it was clear that *Jane Eyre* was in trouble ('healthily alive but in a very unfinished state' was how one local critic tactfully put it) and the Guild announced that instead of moving straight to Broadway the production would extend its tour to Chicago, Pittsburgh, Cleveland and Washington while 'certain difficulties of staging' were ironed out. Interest in Hepburn's return to the stage after her five-year Hollywood absence was however so great that the *New York Times* despatched Brooks Atkinson to Chicago to have a look at *Jane Eyre*, thereby breaking all the then-current rules of what could be reviewed on tour.

Mr Atkinson was not impressed: 'It is to be feared that the current play is only a pedestrian adaptation and Miss Hepburn is not yet the sort of trouping actress who can mould a full-length performance out of scrappy materials. Towards the end her personal reticence begins to emerge as monotony of voice and characterisation, and when the play is finished you have, accordingly, no feeling that anything vital has happened'.

Faced with that verdict from Broadway's most powerful critic, Hepburn saw no point in taking the play onto his home territory: she had no desire to repeat the experience of *The Lake*, and though both she and the Guild thought that in the right circumstances she could make a very strong return to the stage, they saw no reason to ruin that chance in advance with another critical failure. Instead they settled for a highly profitable tour grossing well over three hundred thousand dollars before a graceful closure in Washington, by which time Hepburn had acquired an altogether new interest in her private life.

While *Jane Eyre* was playing in Chicago, observant reporters noticed that there was another character on the tour, though not in the cast. A thirty-two-year-old oil millionaire, film producer and airman called Howard Hughes had been flying his private plane (which had just set a new transcontinental record by getting from Los Angeles to Newark in seven and a half hours) from town to town to be with Hepburn, who he had started seeing in California the previous summer. It seems to have been a brief and passionate affair sharply disapproved of by Kate's friends and family, who reckoned that she was slumming intellectually if not financially. Nevertheless, rumours of a possible marriage were so strong that a huge crowd waited in the snow for hours outside the Chicago County Clerk's office on 21 January 1937 after word had spread that Hughes was about to apply for a marriage licence. He never did, and the affair fizzled out with the *Jane Eyre* tour, leaving Hepburn to spend a long family summer in Connecticut considering her future: it was not a very happy prospect.

*'If I can act, I want the
world to know it; if I can't,
I want to know it'*

7

HEPBURN WAS NOW TWENTY-SEVEN AND IN THE last five years had made twelve films for RKO of which only the first four could really be considered successful; she'd been through one marriage, the Hayward and Hughes affairs, a Theatre Guild tour and a brief Broadway career which had started promisingly, hit one major flop and was now in a kind of abeyance until somebody could come up with a script that would be acceptable.

The hoped-for return to Broadway in triumph with *Jane Eyre* having been denied her, and the Theatre Guild having nothing else immediately on offer, she decided to return to Hollywood in the autumn of 1937 despite the fact that there seemed nothing (and nobody) to go back for; what she couldn't have known was that whatever trouble she was in professionally was as nothing compared to the trouble that RKO were in. Ann Harding, Constance Bennett and Irene Dunne had all left the studio: Ginger Rogers was still there, but had not yet been tried in anything except the Fred Astaire musicals, and among the newcomers only Joan Fontaine was showing real signs of promise. Pandro Berman still needed Hepburn more than she needed him, and almost as soon as she got back from the summer he gave her a new four-picture contract, one which inspired Hepburn to take out a long lease on Fred Niblo's mansion in Beverly Hills. Typically, across half a century of almost constant work there, Kate never once bought a house in California: home was always in the East, at her family house in Connecticut or her own town house in New York. 'I never bought a house in Hollywood' she said simply 'because I never really thought I'd stay.'

But though the new contract was extremely generous, guaranteeing her a hundred and fifty thousand dollars a film, both Hepburn and Berman agreed that they would now have to proceed with a great deal of caution. Three costume flops in a row, immediately preceded by *Sylvia Scarlett*, had not left her exactly high on the box-office popularity charts: indeed she was not to get into the top ten until 1969, almost forty years after her first film, and then only at number nine. In the meantime, she and Berman agreed, the first thing was to get back into modern dress and preferably into a comedy: at first they even considered *The Mad Miss Manton*, a lacklustre farce about a debutante discovering a dead body during a treasure hunt. Wisely they left that one as a career setback for Barbara Stanwyck and moved on to something vastly more promising: a play by George Kaufman and Edna Ferber called *Stage Door* which had been a hit of the 1936 Broadway season for Hepburn's old romantic rival Margaret Sullavan but for which the screen rights were now available to RKO and, therefore, Kate herself. At once, she realised what they had got here: another surefire backstage saga to follow the *Morning Glory* with which she had won her Oscar. Certain changes were made in the script (virtually every line, claimed Kaufman, though not surprisingly since his original had been violently anti-Hollywood) and the director Gregory La Cava decided the film might as well capitalise on the undoubted similarities between Kate and her screen character. Both were rich, overconfident, awkward girls who went in at the Broadway deep end and only then started to learn to swim. To underline the point, the play that we see Hepburn doing in the film of *Stage Door*, though it is called *Enchanted April*, is in fact a thinly-veiled version of *The Lake* with its famous line 'The calla lilies are in bloom again', one that was to become a trademark in Hepburn imitations for years to come.

But there was one great difference between *Stage Door* and Hepburn's other Broadway movie *Morning Glory*: where that had been an uninterrupted solo-star turn, this time RKO were careful to hedge her around with a number of other strong players, not least Ginger Rogers (who got co-starring billing), Lucille Ball, Adolphe Menjou, Constance Collier, Eve

'*Stage Door* brings Katharine Hepburn right back to the spot she occupied before a series of monotonous performances dimmed the memory of *Morning Glory*. It also brings new laurels to Ginger Rogers and Adolphe Menjou, and under the expert guidance of Gregory La Cava cinemagoers should welcome the return of Miss Hepburn from farthingales and tippets.'
New York Times

Arden, Ann Miller and Andrea Leeds. For the first time, Kate was now just part of a winning team rather than its star player, and though she did a wonderful parody of her early stage self it was Andrea Leeds as her suicidal rival who wound up with the Oscar nomination.

To anyone who knew anything about the reality of Hepburn's hesitant Broadway career, *Stage Door* was a joyous succession of in-jokes: Menjou even modelled his director figure on Jed Harris. But La Cava and Berman were careful to make a film which would work on other levels too, and which would repeat the success of *Morning Glory* even it it did mean having Menjou tell Hepburn yet again after a triumphant first night that 'You're an actress now – you belong to the people'. Given the repetitive script and casting, it might have been possible to fall asleep halfway through *Morning Glory* and wake up four years later halfway through *Stage Door* convinced you were still seeing the same movie.

But few things succeed in the cinema quite as reliably as straight repetition, and *Stage Door* was a triumph for the RKO team: 'Since *Little Women* and with the exception of *Alice Adams*' (noted the *Motion Picture Herald*), 'Miss Hepburn has always appeared either as the suffering woman or in costume pictures. This time her role bears a marked resemblance to the one with which she won her Oscar for *Morning Glory* in 1933. A realisation has now come to Miss Hepburn that her popularity has ebbed and with that has come a determination to recoup her lost prestige.'

Along with that lost prestige, Kate also recovered a sense of comedy with *Stage Door* and it was that which was now to lead her into a renewed three-picture partnership with her old partner in crime from *Sylvia Scarlett*, Cary Grant. The first of these was *Bringing Up Baby*, the baby in question being a leopard belonging to poor-little-rich-girl Hepburn who decides also to start playing around with absent-minded paleontologist Cary Grant. Partially remade forty years later by Barbra Streisand as *What's Up Doc?*, Howard Hawks's classic comedy started out being loved by everybody except its audiences: Grant was low on the list of possible stars (Ray Milland, Leslie Howard, Fredric March and Robert Montgomery had all been considered ahead of him) and was nervous at playing 'an intellectual type' until Hawks told him all he had to do was look like Harold Lloyd. Hepburn for her part thought that playing comedy entailed laughing a lot, until rapidly disabused of that notion by an extremely astute Hawks who had seen the mileage there would be in converting a once-prissy classical heroine into a madcap heiress. The very fact that Kate brings to *Bringing Up Baby* a kind of earnestness unknown to Carole Lombard, an earnestness matched by Cary Grant's bemused despair, is what makes it work so well: and fifty years later it remains her picture because, as Otis Ferguson first noted, 'she is breathless, sensitive, headstrong, triumphant in her illogic and serene in the boundless, brassy nerve possible only to the very, very well bred.'

Hawks spent a lot of his time teaching Hepburn the elements of screen comedy, the extreme seriousness with which it needs to be done, but he still found her more than a little noisy on the set. One morning he told her to shut up: 'Katie beckoned me over and told me she had a lot of friends on the set and that I wasn't to talk to her that way or there would be trouble. I looked up the scaffold overhead where there was an electrician, and I said to him "If you had the choice of dropping a lamp on Miss Hepburn or me, who would you drop it on?" and he said "Move out of the way, Mr Hawks". From that time on we got along beautifully, no trouble at all.'

Not everybody was equally devoted to Hepburn: once, rehearsing for *Jane Eyre*, she asked for screens to be put around her on the stage so that she could not be seen at work by prying eyes, an explanation totally rejected by George Kaufman who said 'It's just so that she won't catch Acting' and there were still many allergic to her talents, including, it has to be said, large sections of the American public. And though *Bringing Up Baby* brought her some of the best reviews she was ever to have ('undoubtedly the craziest, wackiest and screwiest farce that has ever been saved from becoming idiotic by the talents of a delightful actress') it also served to highlight a now strongly vocal anti-Hepburn chorus led by Frank S. Nugent of the *New York Times*: 'To the Radio City Music Hall yesterday came a farce which you can barely hear above the precisely enunciated patter of Miss Katharine Hepburn and the ominous tread of deliberative gags. In *Bringing Up Baby*, Miss Hepburn has a role which calls for her to be breathless, senseless and terribly, terribly fatiguing. She succeeds, and we can be callous enough to hint that it is not entirely a matter of performance.'

For a long time now, Hepburn had been told by the magazine gossips that she was 'ruining her own career' by refusing to play a more orthodox Hollywood studio game, and it was left to such vocal defenders as Cukor to point up the notion that it was not a matter of Hepburn growing up to Hollywood, but a matter of Hollywood growing up to Hepburn. Now however attack came from a totally new quarter. Despite generally glowing reviews and good New York business, *Bringing Up Baby* did very badly on its first release across the rest of the United States, the general opinion being that it was too fast, too sophisticated, too supercilious for the average filmgoer. Hawks was firm in his defence of Hepburn: 'She has an amazing body – like a boxer. It's hard for her to make a wrong turn. She's always in perfect balance: she has that beautiful co-ordination that allows you to stop and make a turn and never fall. This gives her an amazing sense of timing: I've never seen a girl that had that odd rhythm and control'; but others were not so sure, least of all Harry Brandt, spokesman for the Independent Theater Owners of America.

'There has long been a delusion abroad that Miss Hepburn's dramatic talent was confined to a narrow range, and her recent costume pictures seemed to prove it. In *Bringing Up Baby* however, she leaps bravely into a new and daffy domain already conquered by Carole Lombard . . . this is undoubtedly the craziest, wackiest and screwiest farce that was ever saved from becoming idiotic by the talent of a delightful actress. Mr Grant and Miss Hepburn, when in doubt, fall flat on their faces, trip over logs, knock each other down. Too farcical? Perhaps; but what joyous, unrestrained, sidesplitting fun. The part of a spoiled playgirl is perfectly suited to Miss Hepburn's talents, and she offers as breezy a performance as the script permits.'
New York Herald Tribune

86

Mr Brandt had never liked the system whereby Hollywood made the films and New York then told people what to think of them; he had long maintained that producers and critics alike were out of touch with 'real America', and soon after his point seemed to have been proved by the nationwide commercial failure of *Bringing Up Baby*, he gleefully published a list of those artists whom he considered to be 'box-office poison' on the evidence of recent movies and their takings. It was in fact an immensely distinguished listing: Garbo, Joan Crawford, Marlene Dietrich, Fred Astaire and Mae West were all on it, and at its head was Hepburn.

That alone might not have much mattered, since Mr Brandt had about as much studio authority as the kind of fashion designer who annually publishes a 'Worst Dressed' list: but Hepburn's listing coincided with a very much more serious realisation about her by RKO.

Like Dietrich, Kate had always been a star more honoured in Europe than on her local territory, and Berman had always been able to console himself with the thought that her films would make up in foreign revenue what they lacked at home. Now however, with the war only a year or two away, Europe was becoming an increasingly tricky sales area for American films and Hepburn's overseas income no longer counted for very much.

So, amazing as it seemed at the time, RKO, having fervently and loyally supported Hepburn through some very thin years, now used the excuse of the Brandt blacklist to throw her to the wolves at precisely the moment when she had made for them one of the most distinguished comedies in the history of the cinema. In view of the relative commercial failure of *Bringing Up Baby*, Berman announced that Hepburn's next picture would be a low-budget B-to-Z programme filler called *Mother Carey's Chickens*.

As ritual public humiliations go, Berman must have known that this one was a winner: within hours Hepburn was in his office brandishing a cheque for two hundred thousand dollars with which to buy out what was left of her RKO contract. Asked if she cared about being labelled 'box-office poison', she said she would start weeping just as soon as she could stop laughing. And, as usual in times of crisis, she went back to Cukor: but this time, with an idea of her own.

Back in 1928, exactly ten years earlier, it may be recalled that she had been understudying Hope Williams in a Broadway comedy of high-society life called *Holiday*. This had then been bought for the screen and filmed in 1930 by Ann Harding, but Hepburn had always kept a proprietorial eye on it and she knew that the remake rights were now with Columbia, a skid-row company who could ill afford to do it justice with any of their own contract people. Despite the charges of 'box-office poisoning', they were however prepared to pay Hepburn a hundred and seventy-five thousand dollars, rather more than she'd been getting at RKO, if she'd come across to them for just that one picture bringing a little prestige with her: Columbia already had the audiences – what they wanted now was critical approval, and Hepburn could usually deliver that.

Holiday had tremendous sentimental value for Kate; it was after all a scene from this which she had used for her first-ever screen test, the one that had led Cukor to cast her in *Bill of Divorcement*, and now that they were starting on their fourth film together she had once again a career to build from the ashes of her RKO contract. Moreover it was a Philip Barry script, and Barry alone among American dramatists of the period wrote the kind of brittle, elegant, idle-rich satires at which Hepburn was always to excel. Believing strongly in a 'family' of players, she and Cukor again approached Cary Grant with whom they had worked so happily

in *Sylvia Scarlett*. He was to play the carefree Johnny Case, who gets engaged to the spoilt daughter of an infinitely wealthy family but winds up in love with her younger sister (Kate) and the conviction that there is more to life than making money. That message might have seemed revolutionary enough when the play was first seen just prior to the Wall Street crash: by 1938 when *You Can't Take It With You* had just won an Oscar for Frank Capra, it seemed already a little dated. However Donald Ogden Stewart, who as an actor had appeared in the original Broadway production that Kate understudied, now came up with a screenplay of considerable charm and wit and it is arguable that this is the first film in which Hepburn truly comes into her own. Here she is working with a director she loved and a co-star she admired in a script about precisely the kind of wealthy Eastern-seaboard freethinkers whom she most understood, and the result was magical: surrounded by a splendid cast (not only Cary Grant but Lew Ayres, Edward Everett Horton, Binnie Barnes, Henry Daniell and Doris Nolan), placed in sumptuous settings and clothes and given some marvellous dialogue, Hepburn had come back into her own territory and triumphed.

This was indeed 'the new Hepburn' so carefully billed on the posters by Columbia, presumably to distinguish her from 'the old Hepburn' who was supposed to be such 'box-office poison'. The only trouble was that *Holiday* had been a one-picture deal and 'the new Hepburn' now had nowhere to go: 'My career seemed to have ended with *Holiday*, I couldn't get a job for peanuts.'

Despite the fact that in *Holiday*, as Pauline Kael later noted, 'her wit and non-conformity made ordinary heroines seem mushy, and her angular beauty made the round-faced ingenues look piggy and stupid. She was hard when they were soft in head and body' or perhaps just because of that very unfashionability, Hepburn now seemed uncastable at the very moment when there loomed on the horizon the one part

she wanted to play more than any other. Lillie Messenger, the RKO talent scout who had first recommended her for *Bill of Divorcement*, had come across the manuscript of a novel called *Gone With The Wind* and had given it to Kate to read, thinking she'd be right for Scarlett O'Hara. Kate agreed, but RKO seemed to have no interest in the book (or indeed her) and Selznick, who did want to make the movie, did not want to do it with Hepburn who in his view 'has two strikes against her – first, the unquestionable and very widespread public dislike of her at the moment, and second the fact that she is yet to demonstrate that she possesses the sex qualities which are probably the most important of all the many requisites of Scarlett'.

Kate retorted that Selznick's taste in 'sex qualities' might well not correspond to those of the world at large, and at the insistence of George Cukor (who was then thought likely to direct) her name was added to a Scarlett short list which also featured Jean Arthur, Loretta Young, Joan Bennett and Paulette Goddard.

Alone among them, Hepburn refused to test on the understandable grounds that as Cukor and Selznick had been the ones to bring her out to California a decade earlier and as she had worked for one or other of them almost ever since, they ought by now to know her on-camera capabilities well enough. Early in November 1938 she was still being listed as a possibility: three weeks later Selznick (still without his Scarlett) had started the burning of Atlanta and his agent brother Myron had brought a young English client to watch. Her name was Vivien Leigh.

With the loss of Scarlett, and the relative commercial failure of the *Holiday* she had so much enjoyed, Hepburn decided that her life in Hollywood was over: no studio seemed in need of her services, she was apparently no longer bankable even in high-society comedies let alone costume dramas, and with Cukor and Selznick now actively engaged on *Gone With The Wind* she had no power-base from which to suggest a new project. Fast approaching her

Right, Hepburn poses fo
Hurrell, Hollywood, 193

thirtieth birthday, unmarried and alone, she went back to her parents in Connecticut to spend a long time thinking about what she should do next.

That was also the winter when the Hepburn family's holiday home on the Connecticut River was washed away in a flash flood, and it began to seem even to the remarkably resilient Kate that somebody somewhere was out to get her. There was however still one figure on the horizon, and it was a friendly one: after their reunion for the refilming of *Holiday*, Philip Barry had gone to see Hepburn in Connecticut with the outlines of two new plays either of which, he said, he'd be happy to develop for her. One was a drama about a diplomat on the brink of suicide which Kate rejected outright, but the other was a comedy about a Philadelphia heiress and three suitors – a play set so firmly in Barry's beloved high society that the eventual musical of it was called just that.

Here, Hepburn thought, was a script that might re-establish her on Broadway and thereby give her a route back to Hollywood on her own terms: Barry was the first to admit that the play still needed a great deal of work, however, and suggested that Hepburn should do it with him at his home on the Atlantic coast of Maine. There, with his star standing over his typewriter, Barry began to custom-tailor the character of Tracy Lord according to certain very definite Hepburn demands: 'Although I'd had a run of failures, I didn't want to go crawling back to a Broadway audience looking for sympathy or affection, nor did I want a big-star entrance which might in the circumstances have been asking for trouble. I just wanted the curtain to go up and find me on stage in a nice dull scene being rude as usual to my mother, so they could all see that I wasn't trying to creep back to popularity but being just as horrible as ever, even though I couldn't get a job anywhere else and everybody out there must have known it'.

Barry wrote to that specification, but he also wrote a lyrical and marvellously durable

'Miss Hepburn skips through *The Philadelphia Story* (in company with Joseph Cotten) in any number of light moods . . . her finely chiseled face is a volatile mask. If it is difficult to take one's eyes off her on stage, it is because she is also blessed with an extraordinary personality. Slim and lovely as she is, Miss Hepburn likewise possesses a voice which in her emotional scenes can be sheer velvet.' *John Mason Brown*

comedy about sex, money and love perfectly tailored to the actress whom, as George Jean Nathan noted, 'he spent two long months observing at close quarters, recording carefully every attractive gesture she made, every awkwardly graceful movement of her body, every odd little quirk of her head and every effective dart of her eye, then to incorporate them all into the play he was writing for her. A line was interpolated to allow her to swing her lithe figure across the stage; another was so contrived that a toss of her lovely brown hair would pictorially embellish it; still another was so framed that it would permit her, while seated, relevantly to cross her knees and display her pretty legs to the critical professors out front. If her voice was found unable to cope properly with a line, it was altered until she could handle it nicely.'

Few actresses in the entire world history of theatre can ever have had such close attention from a playwright: but once *The Philadelphia Story* was completely tailored to Hepburn, there still remained the problem of who would actually be willing to stage it on Broadway. Kate's friendship with the Theatre Guild made them the obvious producers but, as she was later to recall: 'I didn't know that the Guild had just had an expensive costume flop and was very nearly broke; nor did I know that Phil Barry hadn't had a hit in years. Barry didn't know that I hadn't either, and the Guild didn't know that I was supposed to be 'box office poison'. I didn't even know Barry hadn't got a last act. Nobody knew anything, and that was how we had a hit'.

Because the Guild couldn't afford the total financing even of a one-set small-cast comedy for New York, the backing had to come in quarters: one from them, one from the author, one from Hepburn herself and the fourth quarter from her old and wealthy flame Howard Hughes. Thoughtfully, Hepburn also kept the film rights to herself, though for a while it looked as though *The Philadelphia Story* wasn't even going to make it to Broadway, let alone Hollywood.

Its last act had always been a problem, and when they got to New Haven on the tour Barry himself had to admit that it was not being helped by an arch and deeply self-conscious performance from Kate herself. Though they had hedged her round with an extremely strong cast (Van Heflin and Shirley Booth as the reporters, Joseph Cotten as the once and future husband) this was still Hepburn's evening and not all the conceivable rewriting of the last act that they were still doing would be of any help if she could not lose the stagefright that was making her behave on the set like a terrified deer. By the time they got to Washington, however, the local reviews were getting very good indeed, so good that Hepburn was tempted to repeat her *Jane Eyre* performance and settle for a long tour with no Broadway opening at all. 'Why' she enquired of the Guild, 'when I have a barrow and am selling my fruit very well on the sidestreets, should I go to the market-place where all the other barrows are and where I may not do nearly as well?'

The Guild managed to convince her that sooner or later she had to test herself in New York, however, and *The Philadephia Story* duly opened at the Shubert Theatre on 28 March 1939 with Hepburn in a state of such backstage terror that she walked round and round her dressing-room muttering 'This is Indianapolis *not* Broadway'. She needn't have worried: though as one critic put it, 'there are only two classes in this country, those who think Katharine Hepburn is wonderful and those who cannot see her no matter how hard they look', there was no doubt which class had been out front on opening night. Their spokesman was Brooks Atkinson: 'A strange, tense little lady with austere beauty and a metallic voice, she has consistently found it difficult to project a part across the footlights . . . but now she has surrendered to Mr Barry's new play and she acts it like a woman who has at last found the joy she has always been seeking in the theatre.' Hepburn was home at last.

*'I fear I may be a little
too tall for you, Mr Tracy'*

8

'THE PHILADELPHIA STORY' RAN FOR 415 Broadway performances and took almost a million dollars at the box-office; the subsequent nationwide tour on which Hepburn took it lasted another 254 performances and made just over seven hundred and fifty thousand dollars. Considering that she owned a quarter of it, plus the film rights, Kate had within two years turned her Hollywood defeat around into a quite remarkable success, one which she thought could now re-establish her in films on her own terms. Unfortunately, it wasn't quite as simple as that: studios which had found her arrogant even in defeat did not much relish working with her again now that she had a hit to bargain with, and there was no guarantee that *The Philadelphia Story* could repeat on screen its stage success. Maybe Hepburn was a Broadway lady after all: there were at that time a good many female New York stars, from Lynn Fontanne to Katharine Cornell, who had spectacularly failed to make a Hollywood name for themselves and several movie producers now thought that Kate belonged back East with them forever.

Then again, Philip Barry's plays had seldom made successful films: *Holiday* had barely recouped a slender budget and added to all that there was likely to be a casting problem. Neither Van Heflin nor Jo Cotten were at that time considered big enough stars to carry over into the film, and it was thought that acceptable male Hollywood names might well be unwilling to work with a lady who had only a couple of years earlier been considered 'box-office poison' but who now happened to own the property in which they were being asked to feature.

For all those reasons, studios were not exactly queuing up to recapture Hepburn when she and *The Philadelphia Story* became available to the movies in 1940: there was however one producer, Louis B. Mayer of MGM, who had always had a sneaking regard for Kate and had indeed offered her a long-term contract at five thousand dollars a week when she was at her

lowest Hollywood ebb – an offer Hepburn only refused because it did not come with script approval.

Now, in return for bringing him *The Philadelphia Story*, Mayer was prepared to offer her a contract with that script approval, one which would also give her control of director and leading men. Kate went at once to Cukor, who had seen the play several times on Broadway and even taken the precaution of filming it there to mark precisely where the laughs came. There was, though, a tremendous difference between what was needed for the staging and the filming of Philip Barry, a point that had been clearly made to Hepburn when, at the end of the *Holiday* filming, she ran for the merriment of cast and crew the infinitely stagey test of it she had made to get her first Hollywood job a decade earlier.

Cukor knew however that the necessary changes were in acting style rather than scripting: for the screenplay he again hired Donald Ogden Stewart who had done such an accomplished job on *Holiday* and who now added only one short prologue, showing Hepburn throwing her first husband and his golf clubs out through the front door, an event which has in fact taken place several years before the play opens. For the crucial role of the former husband, Cukor and Hepburn decided to go back to Cary Grant, who now demanded top billing (which Kate conceded for the first time in eight years) and a hundred thousand dollars. For the other crucial role of the male reporter they went to James Stewart, and together they achieved a triple triumph best described twenty years later by Penelope Gilliatt. 'All three give performances of such calm comic judgement that one wonders whether Cukor's legendary reputation as an actress's director does him honour enough. It is true that Katharine Hepburn, cast as a rich girl who thrives on fights and who seems to be marrying her deadneck second husband as some sort of penance for flamboyance, has never seemed more invincible; her

faultless technical sense makes one feel that she could play a scene with a speak-your-weight machine and still turn it into an encounter charged with irony and challenge.

'But Cary Grant as her first husband flourishes under Cukor's direction almost as much. For once, his style of unwounding mockery seems to come out of the character: and though it is partly due to the editing that his glances at his recalcitrant ex-wife are as shrewdly fond as they are, they would never have been thrown at all if it had not been for the atmosphere of trust and intimacy that Cukor palpably creates for his cast. One could not imagine them in a Billy Wilder picture. James Stewart, playing a dryly self-loathing gossip journalist, head perpetually inclined as though he were going through a doorway in some quixotic Tudor cottage, seems to have bloomed in the same way.'

James Stewart got an Oscar for *The Philadelphia Story*, as did Donald Ogden Stewart: Miss Hepburn, somewhat pointedly, did not (it went instead to Ginger Rogers for the vastly inferior *Kitty Foyle*) and there were many who decided that this was 'the revenge of the little people of Hollywood' who had long believed that Hepburn was altogether too arrogant for their or her own good. It was, as usual, Cukor who leapt to her defence. In a statement soon after the Oscar upset, he said, 'The most interesting observation to be made about Miss Hepburn is that fundamentally she has never changed at all, either as the actress I directed in 1932 in *A Bill of Divorcement* or as a person whose rare charm and strength is in her uncompromising individuality. It goes without saying that she has improved as an actress: in 1932, being very young, she lacked experience and therefore technique. In *The Philadelphia Story*, on both stage and screen, she has fully developed and perfected her technique. But that was only the realisation of an ability she always possessed. I have no pedestal for Miss Hepburn. She can be wrong. She can be difficult. We have had our

differences. But in the pictures in which I have directed her she has never at any time been unreasonable. She has had good ideas which she will fight for at the drop of a hat, at the same time as she will freely admit being in the wrong if that happens to be the case. Her reputation for being rude, temperamental and unreasonable is undeserved: she chose a direct line and stuck to it. In 1932 she was shocking Hollywood by wearing slacks, which she considers the most comfortable garment ever invented, driving a station wagon and sitting on curbstones because studios do not provide benches for stars whose feet hurt. These activities today would hardly cause the lifting of an eyebrow: this is merely offered in evidence that Hollywood has at last gained some of the naturalness that Miss Hepburn always had. It is a pleasure to see her back, for screen and stage need her great talent. And nothing can break her spirit: she has never changed in the years that I have known her, and is not likely to change in the future.'

All the same, *The Philadelphia Story* marked the end of an era: it was the last time she worked with Cary Grant, perhaps the last genuinely screwball comedy before the coming of a war which made that particular genre look out of both place and date. And although publicists were eager to claim that Hepburn had somehow been 'mellowed' by her *Philadelphia* success story, Cukor's claim that she was still much the same spiky lady was wonderfully borne out by an on-the-set interview with Hedda Hopper on the last day of the shooting. 'Tell me, Miss Hepburn' asked Hopper, 'in what ways has *The Philadelphia Story* really changed you?' 'Well', snorted Kate, 'for a start I've grown three inches.'

Irritated rather than hurt by the Oscar snub, she considered a return to the theatre: there was a new Philip Barry on the typewriter, the usual muttering of a possible *Saint Joan* or *Peter Pan*, maybe a Shakespeare at last, perhaps even the new Bernard Shaw, *The Millionairess*, which

the author himself was said to be keen for her to try. But in the end Hepburn settled for something very much more predictable: another film for MGM.

A new friend, the writer and director Garson Kanin, had alerted her to a story written by his brother Michael and Ring Lardner Junior about an oddball romance between a female political columnist and a tough sportswriter working for the same paper. Hepburn took it to Joe Mankiewicz, who had been her producer on *The Philadelphia Story*, and together they went to see Louis B. Mayer. Kate outlined the story, and said that MGM could have it for a hundred thousand dollars (to be split between the authors) plus another hundred thousand for her. Oh yes, and she'd need cast and director approval as with *The Philadelphia Story*. Mayer asked her to leave the room while he talked privately to Mankiewicz: after about ten minutes, Joe came out and kissed Hepburn on the forehead. 'I thought' he said, 'I'd just like to kiss the blarney stone.' Mayer had agreed to everything: all they now had to find was an actor to play the sports reporter, and Kate knew what she wanted there too. An actor she had never met, but much admired: Spencer Tracy.

Mr Tracy was at the time on location in Florida for *The Yearling*, but that production was abandoned before Hepburn had time to start thinking of an alternative co-star and thus it was that a couple of weeks later the two of them met at the start of a public and private partnership that was to last for almost thirty years and nine films. 'I fear I may be a little tall for you Mr Tracy,' said Kate, five foot ten in her heels and therefore only an inch shorter than him. It was Joe Mankiewicz who replied 'Don't worry, he'll cut you down to size', and cutting Kate down to size was the key not only to the Tracy/Hepburn partnership (at least in public and on screen) but also to the way that because of this, she could now at least be taken to the hearts of middle American moviegoing audiences.

The proud, arrogant, headstrong Hepburn of the 1930s Philip Barry social comedies was now to be turned by MGM and Tracy into an altogether different creature: still a fighter, perhaps, but one prepared in the final round to be beaten by a man. Kate had met her Petruchio, and the taming of the shrew was about to start.

If there was something fundamentally unattractive and extremely chauvinist about this role-change, it has to be admitted that it was achieved in extremely stylish surroundings: *Woman of the Year* (which three decades later became a Lauren Bacall musical) was a craggily written piece given an extremely competent production by George Stevens, Cukor being unavailable at the time and Stevens being the only other director in town with whom Hepburn could bear to have lunch let alone dinner – indeed it was rumoured that they were having a brief affair at the time she first met Tracy. But what both Hepburn and Stevens realised was that in the relationship of Tess Harding and Sam Craig was the perfect marital partnership, one later spelt out by Hepburn in some detail: 'I think on film we came to represent the perfect American couple. Certainly the ideal American man is Spencer; sports-loving, a man's man. Strong looking, a big sort of head, boar neck, a man. And I think I represent a woman. I needle him, I irritate him, I try to get around him, yet if he put a big paw out he could squash me. I think this is the sort of romantic, ideal picture of the male and female in the United States. I'm always skitting about, and he's the big bear, and every once in a while he turns and growls and I tremble. And every once in a while he turns and says some terrible thing and everybody laughs at me and I get furious. It's very male-female.'

It was also extremely calculated: Hepburn and her professional advisers (Cukor, Stevens and now Garson Kanin as well) had discovered that there was no future for her as a lone woman bucking the system, nor was there much future

'*Woman of the Year* is particularly fortunate in having Miss Hepburn and Mr Tracy teamed for the first time in a film and they have a fine old time. They take turns playing straight for each other, act in one superbly directed love scene, succeed in turning several batches of cinematic corn into passable moonshine. As a lady columnist, she is just right; as a working reporter, he is practically perfect. And for once, strident Katharine Hepburn is properly subdued.' *Time*

LIFE

KATHARINE HEPBURN

JANUARY 6, 1941 10 CENTS
YEARLY SUBSCRIPTION $4.50

for the kind of stylish comedies and dramas in which she had made her name during the 30s. Her best hope for the future lay in being the female half of Tracy-and-Hepburn, and one cannot help wondering how long it took the rather less subtle Tracy to realise the precise extent to which he was now being used in the revitalisation of Hepburn's career. He, after all, could always have survived without her; there is a real doubt whether in 1940 her career could have long survived without him.

In the event, it was Louis B. Mayer who insisted on Hepburn's ritual humiliation at Tracy's hands: originally *Woman of the Year* was to end ambiguously, with the audience uncertain whether or not the two of them were finally getting together again as man and wife. Uncle Louis, in the name of American family sanctity, wasn't having any of that: *Woman of the Year* now ends with Kate in the kitchen attempting, albeit unsuccessfully, to get Tracy his breakfast.

Woman of the Year opened to a sigh of general critical relief: here at last was a Hepburn that men, as represented by Spencer Tracy, could deal with and they rewarded her by being generous to the film, one for which Tracy took top billing and thereby established the precedent for the rest of their partnership. 'Listen chowderhead', he barked at Garson Kanin when Kanin once suggested that perhaps it might be more chivalrous to let the lady go first on the posters, 'a movie isn't a goddam lifeboat.'

By the time they came to shoot the new and schmalzy ending demanded by Mayer, there was no doubt in Stevens's mind at any rate that Tracy and Hepburn were already living together. But she had previously agreed to go back to Broadway with the new Philip Barry play, a thoroughly shaky comedy which even a three-month tour failed to get right, though in the course of it Kate was glad to note that she was doing even better box-office business than Gargantua the Gorilla, star of a touring circus then playing many of the same dates.

After the tour, *Without Love* was in fact withdrawn for six months so that Barry could spend

'*Keeper of the Flame* is an expensive testimonial to Hollywood's inability to face the fact that Fascism might offer itself to the US behind a handsome and disarming face . . . for stars Hepburn and Tracy and all concerned, this is a significant failure.' *Time*

another summer trying to get it right for New York and, equally important, so that Hepburn could get back to her new MGM life with Tracy. For the studio had realised, even after one film, that what they now had here was a team and Metro had always loved a team, be it Garland and Rooney or Powell and Loy or Pidgeon and Garson: there was safety in numbers. Accordingly Hepburn was talked out of her enthusiasm to do *Reap The Wild Wind* for Paramount and urged towards *Keeper of the Flame*, an I. A. R. Wylie novel loosely based (like *Citizen Kane*) on

the William Randolph Hearst story but this time more concerned with his death than his life. Hepburn was to play the Great Man's widow, with Tracy as the crusading reporter determined to expose his Fascist past: Donald Ogden Stewart had done the screenplay, over which MGM had agonised for some time before the bombing of Pearl Harbor made an attack on Fascism suddenly acceptable even to Louis B. Mayer.

Cukor was brought in to direct this, the sixth of his ten Hepburn films, though he was later

'*Stage Door Canteen* **demonstrates the fine war work being done for servicemen by the canteen and on it innumerable sketches and variety acts by hundreds of stars are hung like sparkling jewels . . . Katharine Hepburn has a sequence toward the end with the grieving Cheryl Walker which is as moving in warmth as it is gripping in sentiment.'** *Baltimore Sun*

to admit that it was 'a waxwork affair' lacking either the tension that Hitchcock or the grandeur that Welles might have brought to the subject. Critics were inclined to agree and this was to be the last time that Hepburn, now thirty-three, would attempt to play a glamour girl. Cukor was less than happy with her: 'She was always coming on in something glittering and delivering long theatrical speeches, rather as she had in *Christopher Strong* at the very start of her career.'

Loyal to the last, she then returned to Barry and her promise to take *Without Love* onto Broadway, even though the tour at the beginning of the year had taught her that their chances of another success were very slim indeed. Reviews were predictably lukewarm to terrible, but such had been the strength of affection and anticipation built up in New York by the Hepburn-Barry success of *The Philadelphia Story* that they managed to run on the goodwill for nearly four months, during which time Kate also filmed an appearance as herself comforting a young war bride in United Artists' *Stage Door Canteen*.

She then returned to MGM who, while Tracy was occupied with *A Guy Named Joe* and *The Seventh Cross*, put her into a real curiosity: Pearl Buck's *Dragon Seed*, a not-so-*Good Earth* in which Hepburn, Walter Huston, Akim Tamiroff and Turhan Bey were all required to play Chinese peasants at the time of the Japanese invasion in 1937. Hepburn took the trouble to tape up the corners of her eyelids, but

still managed to look about as Chinese as Mary Queen of Scots in a laughably ill-conceived epic. Following that, she tried to persuade Mayer to let her film Eugene O'Neill's *Mourning Becomes Electra* with Garbo as her mother, but when that foundered on a patent lack of studio (and Garbo) interest she settled happily back with Tracy into the film version of *Without Love*.

As Cukor was once more otherwise engaged, the directing of this one went to the ailing Harold Bucquet who memorably summed up his task as follows: 'Directing Mr Tracy amounts to telling him when you're ready to start a scene. He hasn't let me down yet, and when he does perhaps we'll get acquainted. Directing Miss Hepburn is an altogether dif-ferent matter, for you have to tell her when to stop acting instead of when to start. She is much less economical than Mr Tracy, but his style is now rubbing off on her.'

Observers on the set also noticed that she was getting less officious about what her fellow-workers were doing around her; when, on *Keeper of the Flame*, she had commented on several other performances as well as the way in which the script inaccurately alerted the characters to a conflagration, Cukor had said wearily 'It must be wonderful, Kate, to know all about acting *and* all about fires.' Now it began to look as though she was keeping some of that vast knowledge to herself, and Tracy was generally credited with the creation of yet another New Hepburn.

*'There are things in my life
which I would never
discuss with anyone : I
would never even discuss
them with myself.'*

9

'WITHOUT LOVE' WAS MORE AFFECTIONATELY received as a film than it had been as a play a couple of years earlier, largely because the ever-reliable Donald Ogden Stewart had done a competent salvage job on the original script and the whole shaky edifice was now propped up not only by Spencer Tracy but also in minor comic roles by Lucille Ball, Keenan Wynn and Gloria Grahame. What had been a flawed but intermittently intriguing political piece was now just another Tracy/Hepburn comedy which was, in 1945, exactly what the public wanted. It did however mark the end of Hepburn's professional relationship with Philip Barry.

Privately, the affair with Tracy had now taken root and though hints were occasionally and anonymously dropped in the gossip columns about 'Hepburn's romance with a well-known actor', Spencer was never named, largely in deference to his own wife, a much-admired former actress called Louise Treadwell who had not only brought up their handicapped son but had also opened and run a clinic for similarly afflicted children, those deaf from birth. But contrary to widespread and still current public belief, Mrs Tracy was not the Catholic whose religion forbade Spencer getting a divorce: she was in fact a lifelong Episcopalian. The Catholic whose religion forbade a divorce was Spencer Tracy himself, who despite affairs throughout the 1930s with everyone from Loretta Young through Judy Garland to Olivia de Havilland, resolutely maintained the sanctity of his marriage vows.

Nor, now that he was with Hepburn, was there much pressure from her to get disentangled. 'I have always thought that marriage was a funny sort of institution,' she once said. 'I often wonder if people wouldn't be much better off if they didn't have to sign a document. If you know that somebody can get away, you're usually much more attentive. Sometimes I wonder if men and women really suit each other at all. It's inevitable that they should come together now and again, but how well suited are they to living in the same house? Perhaps they should live next door and visit every now and then.'

Which, for the next twenty-two years until Spencer's death, was precisely how they conducted their affair, maintaining private separate addresses and extreme public caution. Neither was ever what you might call gregarious, Tracy always preferring the company of a few age-old drinking buddies and Hepburn that of the few Californians like Cukor and Donald Ogden Stewart who were able to maintain New York standards of literary and theatrical interests and did not appear to have had their brains fried by all that sun. A life of movie premieres and restaurants was thus not something that Tracy and Hepburn had to forfeit in the name of their love, nor were they the kind of flamboyant self-publicists who kept gossip columnists in business. As long as they kept up outward appearances, and were reasonably civil when occasionally questioned at studio press conferences, they were generally regarded as untouchable and perhaps also fundamentally unenthralling by the gossip press: it was as if Mrs Roosevelt had settled down quietly in her middle-to-late years with Harry S. Truman. Somehow they still wouldn't have been the Kennedys.

But what was interesting about the Tracy/Hepburn partnership was the way that its careful on-screen development actually increasingly belied its off-screen reality. In the films, it is Tracy who is the strong, silent, dominant partner and Hepburn who eventually comes to heel after unsuccessful bids for independence. In reality, those roles were reversed: Tracy was an alcoholic, a desperately insecure, argumentative neurotic whom Hepburn dragged out of bar-rooms and, in 1945, back to the New York stage which he had happily quit for better-paid movies in 1930. Kate however still believed that the stage was what really mattered, and convinced Tracy that he should make his return to the boards in Robert Sherwood's war play *The*

In the 1945 *Without Love*, Tracy and Hepburn played a couple trapped inside a loveless marriage . . . a situation that was by now familiar enough to Tracy in real life, seen left arriving with his wife in New York.

Rugged Path on Broadway. It was not a happy experience, nor one that Tracy ever repeated: night after night, Hepburn would stand in the wings urging him on with a play that he never wanted to do in the first place, and now couldn't wait to leave for the film-studio life that suited him and his talent so very much better.

Back in California, Hepburn alone went into *Undercurrent*, a minor Robert Mitchum – Robert Taylor thriller with a plot full of false leads and unkept promises through which Kate picked her elegant if non-committal way; but the film and its lukewarm critical and public reception only served to underline MGM's Hepburn problem, which was essentially that they only knew what to do with her when she was forming half of a now-beloved team known as Tracy and Hepburn. Throughout the 1940s, right up to *The African Queen* in 1951, her non-Tracy movies were among the most deeply undistinguished of her ever murcurial career: and even those they made together didn't always work out as well as *Woman of the Year*. *Sea of Grass*, for instance, made in 1945 but not

Hepburn without Tracy but with the Roberts Taylor and Mitchum for Vincente Minnelli's 1946 *Undercurrent*: 'an indigestible plot full of false leads and unkept promises, like a woman's magazine serial consumed all at one gulp.' *Time*

released until 1947 because Metro was so unhappy with it, was a catastrophic Elia Kazan western about a cattle baron and his unfaithful wife. Kazan, then still five years away from *Panic in the Streets* and *Streetcar Named Desire*, was not yet strong enough to insist on shooting the picture the way he wanted it – as a kind of Robert Flaherty documentary:

'I wanted to do it in the country, with unknown actors, somewhere full of grass and cattle where men's faces look like old leather, whereas Tracy's face by that time in his life looked like the inside of a melon, all soft and sweet . . . he was a wonderful actor but he did not like horses and horses did not like him, which was a problem as he was supposed to be playing a man who spent most of his time on a horse. He was also rather plump, not a Western type, a little lazy – only able to do things a few times before losing interest in them – a little inert, not fierce at all, rather Irish and sly, very funny, very convivial but not in any way at all like the type he was being asked to portray. Then there was Katharine Hepburn playing the middle-class girl who was supposed to have come out from the East to be his wife. Now she is an upper-class girl who wanted then above all to be a big Hollywood star. She is a most intelligent and very decent person, but every time she went to the bathroom to take a piss in that picture she came out with a different dress. And all the dresses were very nice, but not at all lived in . . . so the effect of the picture was a lot of pretty illustrations. In the first few days we did a farewell scene between Hepburn and Melvyn Douglas who played her lover, and she cried a lot in that and I thought how wonderful, because I had thought she was a cold person. Later I discovered that she cried like that without pretext: if her eggs are cold, she cries . . . but Mayer said the channel of her tears was all wrong: "It goes too close to her nostril, it looks like the tears are coming out of her nose like snot". I said, "Jesus, I can't do anything about the way her tears fall" and he said,

113

'In Elia Kazan's *The Sea of Grass* Mr Tracy is grim, purposeful and occasionally ludicrous while Miss Hepburn remains as pert as a sparrow ... the picture is much too long but there's lots of Western scenery and I suppose the general confusion of the plot isn't any worse than usual.' *New Yorker*

"Young man, you have one thing to learn. We are in the business of making beautiful pictures of beautiful people, and anybody who does not acknowledge that should not be in movies" ... MGM in those days had only three rules. One, never offend anybody. Two, make everybody want to go to the movies. Three, organise the movies as a business. And as soon as you organise art as a business, you're in trouble.'

But if *Sea of Grass* wasn't art, it certainly wasn't business either: John McCarten for the *New Yorker* thought Tracy 'grim, purposeful and ludicrous', Hepburn 'as pert as a sparrow' and Douglas 'as gloomy as if he were playing the wronged husband instead of the dashing lover'. Uneasy in westerns, Metro decided Hepburn might fare better back in one of her old costume dramas: they therefore cast her next as Clara Wieck Schumann in a breathtakingly ter-

rible piano piece called *Song of Love* about starving nineteenth-century composers. Kate did a lot of her own piano-playing but not enough to take viewers' minds off the script, which though written by six credited scenarists appeared to have been assembled overnight on the backs of old pianola rolls.

By now, it was clear that MGM had no more idea what to do with Hepburn as a solo star than had RKO a decade earlier, but her loyalty to Louis B. Mayer was considerable: at a time when more and more stars were beginning to run their own careers, Garson Kanin once asked Kate why she didn't make the break considering what terrible scripts the studio had recently landed her with. 'Ah yes' replied Kate, 'but MGM are really wonderful when you're in Chicago and have to change trains.'

And they did at least stand by her when her

popularity slumped in the late forties to an all-time low: they even stood by her when she campaigned for Henry Wallace (then running against Truman on the 'Progressive' ticket) and when she was one of the first to speak out against the evil Parnell Thomas and his House UnAmerican Activities Committee after it became clear that this McCarthy forerunner was out to get such close friends of hers as Donald Ogden Stewart. Ironically it was a script that Stewart had written for Tracy and Hepburn (*Keeper of the Flame*) which eventually led to his indictment by the Committee and a forced exile to London, where he was to spend the rest of his long life. But Kate's speech on his behalf, and by extension on behalf of all other Hollywood artists falsely accused of national disloyalty, was worthy of one of her own best films: 'J. Parnell Thomas' she announced to an anti-censorship rally at a Los Angeles stadium in May 1947, 'is engaged in a personally conducted smear campaign of the motion picture industry. He is aided and abetted in his efforts by a group of super patriots who call themselves the Motion Picture Alliance for the Preservation of American Ideals. For my part, I want no part of their ideals or those of Mr Thomas. The artist since the beginning of time has always expressed the aspirations and dreams of his people. Silence the artists, and you have silenced the most articulate voice the people have.'

She then joined her old friends George Stevens and David Selznick, as well as Bogart and John Ford, on the anti-McCarthy Committee for the First Amendment and was duly denounced by Leo McCarey and Sam Wood as having raised money for 'a very special political party' though this was undoubtedly that of Henry Wallace, a gentle liberal, rather than anything remotely Communist. Tracy meanwhile stayed as far as possible in the background, muttering that the last time actors got mixed up in politics Abraham Lincoln wound up dead. All the same, both he and Louis B. Mayer were more than a little nervous about the effect of Kate's outspoken politics on her already plummeting career, and it is interesting as well as unnerving to note that when, in late 1947, Spencer signed for *State of the Union*, the Lindsay and Crouse drama about a Presidential candidate being brought back to his political principles by an estranged wife, it was Claudette Colbert who was cast for the obvious Hepburn role of the wife.

Luck, however, was now on Kate's side: on the Friday before shooting was due to start, Colbert presented herself at the office of the producer/director Frank Capra and informed him that in view of her precarious health, her doctor (who also happened to be her husband) had recommended that she leave the set every evening at five o'clock. Capra, a man who liked to work a little later when the mood took him, regretted that would not be possible, whereupon Colbert tore up her contract and left his office.

Capra, who had a studio ready and waiting for his Monday-morning start, rang Tracy in some confusion about the inevitable delay: unnecessary, said Tracy. He had an actress right there at home who had read the script and would be delighted to play it, starting Monday at the agreed time. Quite what would have happened to Hepburn's career, or indeed the on-screen partnership with Tracy, had Colbert not decided to walk out of *State of the Union* (known in Britain as *The World and His Wife* because of the confusion over precisely which union was being referred to) is a matter of conjecture only; as things turned out, Hepburn found herself working for 'a funny, totally concentrated, imaginative and warm creature who felt violently, loved to laugh, and could lead an audience to water and make them drink'. And Capra returned her devoted admiration: 'There

are women and there are women and then there is Kate. There are actresses and there are actresses and then there is Hepburn. A rare professional-amateur, acting is her hobby and her living and her love. She is as wedded to her vocation as a nun is to hers, and as competitive in acting as Sonja Henie was in ice-skating. No clock-watching, no humbug, no sham temperament. If she made up her mind to become a runner, she'd be the first woman to break the four-minute mile.'

Not everyone on that *State of the Union* set shared Capra's devotion to Hepburn, least of all Adolphe Menjou her old co-star from *Morning Glory* and *Stage Door* but now leader of the pro-McCarthy Hollywood Right. 'Scratch a do-gooder like Hepburn' he used to mutter on the set, 'and she'll yell *Pravda*.' 'Scratch a Hepburn' retorted Tracy, 'and what you get is an ass full of buckshot.'

It says something for the diplomacy of Capra and the professionalism of his politically divergent cast that he managed to deliver, on time and under budget, what is for my money the best of all the Tracy/Hepburn pictures: a marvellously acid Washington closed-doors drama in which Capra exposed the workings of American democracy with none of the small-town sentiment that always in my view marred his better-loved *Mr Deeds* and *Mr Smith*. Here we get not only Tracy and Hepburn and Menjou, but Angela Lansbury in her first major role as the society hostess who tempts Tracy away from his principles and Van Johnson as the political columnist in a film which, it was even suggested, taught President Truman how best to campaign for his forthcoming re-election. Certainly he took the trouble to see and applaud the film in Washington when it was being claimed by Menjou and others that the whole *State of the Union* was nothing more than a dirty Communist plot.

The film did no better than most overtly political dramas at the box-office, but its critical success did at last restore the respectability of

'*Adam's Rib* is a rambunctious spoof which again presents Katharine Hepburn and Spencer Tracy as the ideal U.S. Mr and Mrs of upper-middle income. This time, besides being wittily urbane as usual, they are both lawyers . . . Hepburn's elegantly arranged bones and Tracy's assurance as an actor make them worth looking at in any movie, though the chief asset here is a high-toned song called *Farewell Amanda* which Cole Porter must have written while waiting for a bus.' *Time*

the Tracy/Hepburn team after the fiasco of *Sea of Grass*, and Metro were careful then to lead them back towards another safe battle-of-the-sexes comedy. This one, written by another famous off-screen partnership (the actress Ruth Gordon and her husband, the writer-director Garson Kanin) was *Adam's Rib*, a comedy about a husband and wife, both lawyers, who find themselves respectively prosecuting and defending the same client, Judy Holliday, after she has shot her own unfaithful husband. This idea of a legal-marital confusion first captured the imagination of the Kanins when they heard the real-life story of the actress Adrianne Allen who, having divorced Raymond Massey, proceeded to marry the lawyer who had got her the divorce while Massey married the lawyer's ex-wife; by the time it reached the screen however, it had become a classic George Cukor comedy which gently nudged the audience into an awareness that they were perhaps watching something about the off-screen as well as the on-screen Tracy and Hepburn.

One sparkily married couple writing for another couple who had been together everywhere except at the altar for the last seven years inevitably led to a certain amount of truth about partnerships: *Adam's Rib* also served to establish Judy Holliday on screen, since Cukor was determined to prove to Harry Cohn that she alone could transfer her *Born Yesterday* stage success to Hollywood. Most important of all, it was shot on location around New York, still home territory to Hepburn and Cukor and the Kanins, which meant that a number of agile Broadway stage actors like Tom Ewell and David Wayne could be used as a welcome change from the rapidly ageing ranks of MGM's regular Hollywood support casts.

Adam's Rib was therefore a breath of sharply intelligent New York air (it even had a theme song by Cole Porter, who insisted that Kate's name in the film be changed from Madeline to Amanda since the latter was easier to rhyme) and a number of Eastern critics now began to

pick up its nudging hints about the reality of the Tracy/Hepburn relationship: 'their perfect compatability' wrote Bosley Crowther for the *New York Times* 'in comic capers is delightful to see. A line thrown away, a lifted eyebrow, a smile or a sharp, resounding slap on a tender part of the anatomy is as natural as breathing to them and plainly they took great pleasure in playing this rambunctious spoof.'

Adam's Rib ends with the by-now-traditional Hepburn capitulation in the last reel to a finally dominant Tracy, but in their private life she was in fact now about to break free from him for a while. Back in New York for the location shooting of the film, she had suddenly remembered for the first time in almost a decade how much she loved Broadway, how much she still wanted to get back to the live stage he so loathed. Indeed as if to remind her of what she'd been missing, Cukor had shot *Adam's Rib* in an extremely stagey way: there was no escaping the fact that any script part-written by Ruth Gordon was bound to look theatrical, but *Adam's Rib* though conceived as an original screenplay looks more Broadway-based than many of the films that really were.

In any event, when the Theatre Guild now came up with the suggestion that Kate might like to play Rosalind for them in an *As You Like It* revival at the Cort and before that on a cross-country tour, she accepted at once. She was, however, careful to build in a few safeguards: she insisted on an English director from the Old Vic, Michael Benthall, and a three-month period of verse training with the veteran English classical actress Constance Collier who had played with her in *Stage Door* thirteen years earlier. 'The part of Rosalind', Kate told an enquiring journalist, 'is really one of the great tests of how good an actress you are, and I want to find out.' There was another reason she didn't add in public – her mother, then seventy-two and close to death, had always expressed a wish to see her daughter in Shakespeare.

Reviews on the nine-week tour of *As You*

The fair Rosalind, in the 1950 Broadway *As You Like It*: **critics did. Right, '***The African Queen* **is not great art but it is great fun. Essentially it's one long, exciting, old-fashioned chase. Filmed in the Belgian Congo and Uganda by Huston, it tells its adventure yarn in a blaze of Technicolor, fine wild scenery and a lot of action. Bogart does the best acting of his career as the badgered rumpot who becomes a man and a lover against his will. And Hepburn is excellent as the gaunt, freckled, fanatic spinster. Their contrasting personalities fill the film with good scenes, beginning with Bogart's tea-table agony as the indelicate rumbling of his stomach keeps interrupting missionary Robert Morley's chitchat about dear old England'** *London Times*

Like It were ecstatic, both for Kate and for Benthall's production. When they got to Broadway, though one or two critics were less than bowled over ('Miss Hepburn's legs are always poetry' noted John Mason Brown, 'but I cannot help feeling that she mistakes the Forest of Arden for the campus of Bryn Mawr'), public interest in seeing a movie star in Shakespeare (or maybe just in seeing those fabled legs in tights) was such that they chalked up a hundred and forty-five performances.

During the run there was talk that she would stay with the Theatre Guild for another season, possibly to do *The Taming of the Shrew* or even *Hedda Gabler*, but then came the offer of something she found still more intriguing. John Huston and Humphrey Bogart now had the film rights for *The African Queen*, C. S. Forester's 1935 novel about a rough Canadian engineer and a prim Methodist missionary

trapped together on a derelict boat (the 'Queen' of the title) making her way down an African river to escape the Germans of the First World War. Bette Davis and Deborah Kerr had earlier been suggested for Rose Sayer, and when Bogart and Huston went to see Hepburn on behalf of Sam Spiegel, who was producing anonymously after a little local difficulty with the McCarthy Tribunal, there was already a feeling that they were going to war with her rather than just another location. Bogart recalled later: 'John and I had heard all the stories about her. How she drove hard Yankee bargains with producers . . . how she said that Hollywood was only a necessary evil to her while her real interests were the stage and her family home in Connecticut . . . how she wouldn't sign autographs and detested publicity . . . then there was the zany side like the five baths a day she said she took because they

helped her think, and the way she always said 'yah' for 'yes' and 'rally' for 'really' and the way she sweetened tea with strawberry jam and shined her freckled face with rubbing alcohol and never used jewelry or perfume.'

Hepburn too seemed to have her doubts, notably about Huston who in her view 'couldn't hit a tin can with a peashooter but liked to give the impression he could kill an elephant'. Nevertheless she was won over by the script, intrigued by the idea of her first foreign location, reassured to find that Lauren Bacall (the actress, then married to Bogart, who would in later years come most closely to resemble her on stage and did indeed play her old part in the musical of *Woman of the Year*) was also along for the safari. 'If you need me' she told Constance Collier in parting, 'the name is Kate Hepburn, Belgian Congo.'

The location was not, as I suggested at the beginning of this book, an easy one and even after Huston had given Hepburn the 'Mrs Roosevelt' clue to the playing of Rose it still took several days for her to come to terms with his way of shooting and with Bogart's playing of a role she must have considered well within the range of her beloved Tracy.

Later however, when she had recovered from the dysentery which Bogart and Huston both escaped by their decision to drink only Jack Daniels until safely home again, Kate came to regard both Africa and *The African Queen* as 'the great adventure' and one she was determined to survive. The lady whom my father was to describe, back in the English studios of *The African Queen*, as 'one of those curiously lucky aristocrats to whom life comes easily' had decided that Africa and Bogart and Huston and the crocodiles were to be conquered and annexed just as Hollywood and Broadway and Tracy and MGM had been, and along the way she and Bogart discovered that they were making a comedy as well as an escape drama: 'He and she were just very funny together' said Huston, 'one calling forth an unexpected quality in the other, and the combination of their two characterisations brought out the humor in situations which on the printed page hadn't seemed very funny. Suddenly it was the story of a prim spinster becoming captain of a ship'.

Now forty-two and playing fifty-five, Hepburn had the greatest dramatic success of her career with *The African Queen*. Though it would win her none of the three more Oscars that came for later and lesser work (she got the nomination, but was beaten by her old *Gone With The Wind* rival Vivien Leigh for *Streetcar*), it won her the best reviews of her life. 'The duel,' wrote Henry Hart, 'between this woman, as played by Miss Hepburn, and the dirty, amiable ne'er-do-well played by Mr Bogart is a masterpiece of acting, directing and dialogue . . . they have descended the river in order to reach a lake whose far shore is British territory. They are at the end of their tether, and she prays "Oh God, tomorrow, when we are dead, judge us not by our failures but by our love". That is a very powerful line and Miss Hepburn reads it flawlessly. After she has spoken it her strength, her pride and her will are all gone. The back that had once been so straight crumples, and the head that had always been so high dodders to the deck and is still. She has been indeed laid low. One accepts not only her end, but the end of the film. And then the camera lifts up from the deck of the dirty boat, up from the almost lifeless man and woman, up from the swamp reeds and the jungle grass, up from the tops of the tropical trees and there, a few hundred yards away, is the lake. The effect is breathtaking: it is an instance of the perfect utilisation of pure cinema.'

And Hepburn knew that she had been a part of that effect, knew that she had somehow now got beyond the jokey battle-of-the-sexes Tracy comedies, beyond the costume dramas and the old high-society romps. With *The African Queen* she had become for the first time a great dramatic actress.

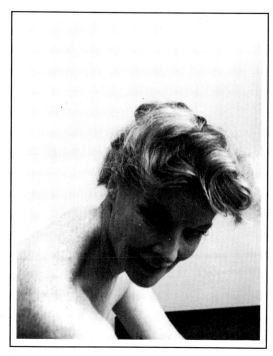

*'She ain't got much
meat on her . . . but what
she's got is cherce'*

10

LIKE 'THE PHILADELPHIA STORY' A DECADE earlier, *The African Queen* was another declaration of Hepburn independence: it meant she didn't need Metro, or Tracy, or Cukor to get her out of trouble and a *Time* cover story began to acknowledge that the press was no longer dealing with just another movie star: 'Her body suggests a collection of fine bones held together by freckles. Her vivid, angular face is topped by red hair pinned up any which way. Her penetrating voice can sometimes be as disturbing as her strong opinions . . . in Kate Hepburn's twenty-four years on stage and screen her detractors have been many, but this year she is stronger than she ever was: by her own estimate she has made more than three million dollars as an actress.'

But part of Hepburn's technique, on screen and off, was to suggest that she really didn't have to do this kind of thing for a living. 'I have never,' she told the astonished hack from *Time*, 'really considered myself an actress. I have always felt that one day I might do something quite different, something in which I won't have to be personally so prominent. It will be something where I don't have to try to sell myself, which is a very humiliating endeavor however well paid. I've always had this strange and strong dream that if I stopped acting and went home to Hartford, I wouldn't be able to remember a thing about my career. Not one damn thing.'

For now, though, it had to be continued: there was one more picture to be made under her 'unwritten' contract with Metro, and Tracy had to be weaned once more from the bottle to which he'd taken heavily when Hepburn left him for Bogart and *The African Queen*. By this time Cukor and the Kanins were back on the scene with another Tracy/Hepburn comedy, though this was already the last on which they were all to work. Called *Pat and Mike*, it told the story of an upper-class golf and tennis champion (Kate) being managed by a crooked promoter (Spencer) who seems to have stepped straight from the pages of a Damon Runyon short story. Having fought their battle of the sexes through journalism (*Woman of the Year*), science (*Without Love*), politics (*State of the Union*) and law (*Adam's Rib*) there was now the feeling that sport would make an obvious follow-up, especially given Hepburn's devotion to tennis – it was indeed watching her on a court that gave Kanin the idea for the story. But efficient and much loved though it was, there was a feeling in *Pat and Mike* that everyone involved was merely going through some extremely accomplished mechanical paces: the Kanins and the Tracy/Hepburn/Cukor team seemed to have said all they really wanted to say about sparring couples, and the use of a lot of professional sportsmen here only served to underline that what might have suited Runyon for one of the many fleeting subplots in *Guys and Dolls* was looking distinctly stretched at ninety minutes. Already, something had ended here: in the next fifteen years Tracy and Hepburn were only to make two more films together, one good and one terrible, and though both were also to work separately with Cukor, the teamwork with the Kanins was now over forever.

As if to mark the end of another period in her professional life, and to shake the dust of MGM off her shoes, Hepburn then flew to London to fulfil a promise she had made to Michael Benthall at the time of their Broadway success with *As You Like It*: that in London, on his home territory, she would play the first major production of Shaw's *The Millionairess*. Written in 1935 for Edith Evans (who declined it), this had the most chequered career of any of Shaw's major plays and had in fact still not been seen in London or New York when Kate came to do it, though it had been extensively toured and it was widely known that Shaw himself (who died only two years earlier) had always wanted Hepburn to play it in America. Her London stage debut (at the New Theatre in June 1952) was thus respectfully received, though, for the *Guardian*, Philip Hope-Wallace thought that:

'Next to *Geneva* this must be Shaw's feeblest play, and it does him scant tribute now to rake up an irresponsible horse-play full of respect for Mussolini and ruthlessness in general ... however it allows Katharine Hepburn a suitable stamping ground for her own brand of exhibitionism. She had been with us in shadow, so to say, ever since the miracle of the talking film brought that harsh, flat, cawing voice into our lives. Reproduced in the flesh it is even flatter, harsher and louder than one had supposed. It seems to have no inflexions, no gradations or variety of any kind and yet, such is Miss Hepburn's strident, domineering stage personality that all these defects are forced to seem to us virtues ... Miss Hepburn is that rare thing, the number-one size star personality, and everything she chooses to do is right if only because it works so triumphantly on the audience. We are not merely bounced into accepting, we are bulldozed into belief.'

Benthall had hedged her round with a very

strong London cast (Cyril Ritchard, Robert Helpmann, Meriel Forbes) but this was still very much Hepburn's evening: 'her performance' noted Harold Hobson 'like the Grand Canyon, the Taj Mahal and the two-headed pig is quite something; and she speaks the last noble speech on marriage absolutely beautifully with, at one point, a trembling hesitation about the mouth and a catch of the breath that are moving to a point unusual in Shaw.' This was also the time when a young Kenneth Tynan recognised in Kate one of those high-definition performers that he was always greatly to admire: 'Miss Hepburn is not versatile; she is simply unique. She glitters like a bracelet thrown up at the sun. Like most stars of real magnitude she can do one or two of the hardest things in the world supremely well, and *The Millionairess* scores a bullseye on the target of her talents. It is just hard enough for her, just close enough to impossibility: Epifania is written on one note, but it is Miss Hepburn's note and she makes it into a cadenza. As an actress, she has sex but no particular gender: her masculinity appeals to women, and her sexuality to men. Only to Garbo and Dietrich is that also true.

'At close quarters', Tynan added, 'Hepburn looks as if she would be warm to the touch, ready and willing to communicate. To the tip of her nose she is pink; her nostrils shine as if oiled, and the bright bone of her cheeks stretches the skin. You can see the wrinkles round her eyes, but the sun's dazzle has set them there; they enclose the alertness, the appetite for life which her admirers prize. Her build is pencil-slim and capable, and her hair, a wiry flourish of chestnut, is dragged back into a knot ... she talks about that generation of Hollywood stars which time seems to have ignored: she admires the invulnerability of Cagney and Bogart and Tracy and Bette Davis, finding in them a diamond core which could not be dimmed or devalued: they were Stars. "And why" she asks, suddenly mad "should actors pretend they're like other people when they're not?".'

For Stephen Tennant, Hepburn adulation went even further: 'She is that yell, that shriek that is simultaneous with the bell ringing at school, the bell that signifies books clapped together, pencils thrown down, and the rush into the playground for the break.' But however ecstatic the British were (as always) to be about one of those very rare American film stars whom they generally wished had been born on their own side of the Atlantic, *The Millionairess* team were in for a nasty shock when they got to Broadway with the same production in the November of 1952. New York critics had already welcomed Kate back to the boards a couple of years earlier in *As You Like It*; now they were less than pleased to see her back again in a relatively minor work. 'The plan' wrote Brooks Atkinson for the *New York Times* 'seems to be for Miss Hepburn to supply the youth and vitality and in this maundering script she knocks down anything that gets in her way, but so much energy and caterwauling can be stupefying for a full evening.' Walter Kerr in the *Herald Tribune* added 'Miss Hepburn is beautiful, radiant, vital and not very good. At times she sounds like an alarm clock that nobody can switch off . . . she doesn't walk, she marches. She doesn't speak to other characters, she clutches them in a vice-like grip . . . and when she has to get off a sofa, she simply throws her feet into the air and lands on them. I had expected Miss Hepburn to bring to the parched and impoverished realism of our contemporary acting styles a refreshing rain. Last night seemed like a deluge.'

For the critic of the *Journal American*, her performance was one of 'amateur mugging, bombast and elephantine coyness: if it was a tour de force, I get the force but I don't dig the tour.'

Faced with that kind of critical onslaught, one which would have closed most Broadway shows overnight, Hepburn still managed to get ten New York weeks out of *The Millionairess*

Summertime (or *Summer Madness*) **and the canal pratfall that was to leave her with a permanently weeping eye: 'Miss Hepburn has laboured long in the service of her art, and like a great many grand-actress personalities she has now created herself in her own image. Everything superfluous is gone, the elements are refined and complete—the sad mouth, the head-back laugh, the snap of chic in shirtmaker dresses, the dream of enchantment behind wistful eyes, the awakened puritan passion of the girl in love, the regular way with children, the leggy stride, and always the bones—those magnificent, prominent, impossible bones once described as the greatest calcium deposit since the white cliffs of Dover.'** *Saturday Review*

and her enthusiasm for Shaw's script was still so radiant that she then spent several months closeted with the director Preston Sturges trying to get a film treatment together. Kate's hope had been that, as with *The Philadelphia Story*, she could then sell this and herself back to Hollywood as a package, but the studios in California had never been much interested in Shaw and the one London-based producer who had made the filming of his plays a speciality (Gabriel Pascal) was by now out of the business altogether. When *The Millionairess* was eventually filmed, ten years later with Sophia Loren, the result was so catastrophic that one yearned to see what the Hepburn/Sturges version might have been like. It certainly couldn't have been worse.

Depressed by Hollywood's unwillingness to let her do *The Millionairess*, unwilling to do yet another battle-of-the-sexes comedy with her beloved Tracy, and unsure now how welcome she was on Broadway, Hepburn spent almost the whole of the next year in a state of suspended animation. There was a vague theory that she might do another film for John Huston (his own adaptation of *Miss Hargreaves*, the tale of a seventy-year-old English lady who scandalises a conservative cathedral town) but when financing for that proved unavailable she pottered around looking after Tracy and thinking how curious it was that even after a couple of hits the size of *The African Queen* and *Pat and Mike* she still could not command enough studio attention to get *The Millionairess* shot: 'That was the greatest professional disappointment of my life. Sturges and I had done one of the funniest scripts ever written but he was over the hill, my career was as always in the trembles, and people just wouldn't finance us . . . the failure of that project was what killed Preston. He died of neglect.'

Hepburn, as usual, survived and early in 1954 another director she much admired, David Lean, sent her a play by Arthur Laurents called *Time of the Cuckoo* about a mousey secretary

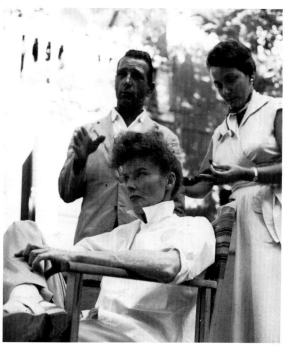

from the midWest who goes to Venice in search of romance and finds it in the shape of a suave, if married, Italian. Though by no means the best of Laurents' many scripts, this one has proved surprisingly durable and was to reappear on Broadway years later as a Richard Rodgers-Stephen Sondheim musical called *Do I Hear A Waltz?* In the meantime however David Lean, whose *Brief Encounter* had established him in 1945 as the master director of clenched, bittersweet love stories with downbeat endings, had with H. E. Bates made a screen adaptation of it called variously *Summertime* (in the US) and *Summer Madness* (in the UK) and wanted Hepburn to play the spinster opposite Rossano Brazzi.

That she did, bringing to an otherwise not hugely distinguished film her customary touch of class and distinction: it was left to the critic of the *Saturday Review* to note that regardless of its performances or the way the script had been pared down from Laurents' more subtle and complex original, 'as a movie *Summertime* does exactly what movies were supposed to do when Edison first invented the darn things. It brings to you, through the magic of the camera, all the glory of a famous city thousands of miles away.' Though it won no Oscars, the cast and crew all deserved special awards from the Venice Tourist Board, none more so than Hepburn who did without a double that famous backwards fall into a heavily polluted Canal. But she failed to mask her eyes sufficiently and has consequently for the last thirty years suffered from a constant-weeping affliction. It seems a high price to have paid for a minor-comedy pratfall.

The Venice filming over, Kate stopped in London on her way home to Tracy and California, only to be tempted into another stage project and this perhaps the most adventurous and distinguished of her entire career. Michael Benthall, her *As You Like It* and *The Millionairess* director, was now in charge of the Old Vic and planning a major tour of Australia with her

The Millionairess co-star Robert Helpmann. Would Kate, the two men enquired, like to join them at the head of a company which would be touring the length and breadth of Australia in 1955 with *The Taming of the Shrew, Measure for Measure* and *Merchant of Venice?* Kate would. Though the original friendship between her and Benthall and Helpmann had been a tricky one, largely because *As You Like It* had been Benthall's first non-Helpmann success and the actor felt he was somehow being eased out of the director's affections by the actress, there had later grown up a strong bond between Helpmann and Hepburn when they were playing *The Millionairess*: 'She used to take me for weekends to a house she had at Sayborough in Long Island Sound. By this time it was winter and there were no servants, only this silent creature and me. I was the Caliban who carried the wood . . . then she took me home for Christmas dinner. There were seventeen of them and I was the only one who wasn't either a Hepburn or married to one. Kate had taken over the matriarchal position.'

Having agreed to play Portia, Katherina and Isabella on a six-month tour that would take in Sydney, Melbourne, Brisbane, Adelaide and Perth, Hepburn went back to the careful Shakespearian coaching of Constance Collier, the actress whose retirement she had been paying for these past ten years and who in return was more responsible than anyone for getting Kate safely onto the boards in *As You Like It* and *The Millionairess*. But Collier was now seventy-seven and dying: she did however bequeath to Hepburn one final and invaluable gift – a secretary, Phyllis Wilbourn, who has been with Kate ever since.

On arrival in Australia, perhaps aware of how much the tour meant to Helpmann (who was returning home) and might mean to the finances of the Vic, Hepburn went out of her way to be charming to the journalists she usually loathed. She even gave a press conference at which she tactfully fielded questions about Helpmann's sexual interests, her own, and why she always dressed so appallingly ('Because' she said, 'as Dorothy Gish once remarked, if one is paid to dress up in working hours there really is no need to do it in free time.') She also graciously answered questions about what time she arose, what she ate for breakfast and whether she was temperamental ('Not at all. Look at how charming I am being: of course, I may drop dead at any minute.')

Even so, the Australians were determined not to be too impressed: critics in Sydney compared Hepburn's Shakespearean performances unfavourably to those of Vivien Leigh and Diana Wynyard (the last two female stars who had been sent out by the Vic) and when they got to Melbourne there was a banner headline announcing that the only reason they were there was that Hepburn's career as a Hollywood star was now as dead as Helpmann's career as a dancer in London.

Still, audiences flocked to see them and Hepburn, undaunted as ever by a bad press, became a manic tourist, forcing Helpmann to rise at dawn in search of the lyrebirds that he had almost managed to forget from his childhood. Australia appealed to the pioneer and the great outdoorswoman in Kate and she enjoyed looking at it, if anything, even more than the Australians enjoyed looking at her.

Passing through London yet again on her way home, she had agreed to play opposite Bob Hope in a dire remake of *Ninotchka* called *The Iron Petticoat*, certainly the worst of all her postwar films and arguably the worst that she ever made. But now she had much more to worry about than just another temporary slump in her moviemaking: during her prolonged absences on Broadway and in the West End and Australia, Tracy had gone back to the bottle, and was now in such a bad way physically and alcoholically that he was actually taken off a picture called *Tribute to a Bad Man* and replaced with James Cagney. MGM, sensing the beginning of the end, sensitively cancelled Tracy's contract and gave him a small pension.

That was more than enough to alert Kate to her domestic responsibilities: returning immediately to California from the tatters of *Iron Petticoat* she dried Tracy out, nursed him back to sufficient health for *The Old Man and the Sea* and then made a point of never leaving him again, whether he was working or not, for long enough to allow him back to the drink. She therefore trailed him through the tricky Hemingway locations, and no doubt could in a crisis have taken over the role of the Old Man herself. Back in Hollywood while Tracy was doing the studio sequences, she then went into *The Rainmaker* opposite Burt Lancaster: this was the Broadway and London stage hit about a 'prairie Cinderella' (Hepburn) whose confidence in herself is boosted by the arrival of a travelling con-man who can apparently make even rain fall. 'A slight, whimsical piece' thought Lindsay Anderson, 'well, if stagily presented, but let's face it, Katharine Hepburn is not a shy, coltish twenty-eight. She is a mature

and intelligent actress of commanding
presence, and though she does as well as she can
with *The Rainmaker* I found it embarrassing.'

But as she now could not leave Tracy for
long, and as the two of them still nurtured a
deep neurosis about being seen together in
public unless they were actually working
together, what they obviously needed was
another joint film.

Unhappily neither Cukor nor the Kanins had
anything on offer, and the one they ended up
with was a thoroughly shaky little William
Marchant comedy called *The Desk Set* (and in
England more descriptively *His Other Woman*)
for which Hepburn once again did her spinster-
into-bride routine while Tracy stood around
looking craggy.

Quite apart from *The Desk Set*, Hepburn
now had a considerable problem: she couldn't
leave Tracy or California for long, but on the
other hand she still had a career of her own to
consider – one which was being not much
helped, and was in danger of being considerably
harmed, by the kind of rubbishy comedies into
which she'd recently fallen by accidents of con-
venience. Hollywood seemed to have nothing
of any interest for her to do except look after
Tracy, and she couldn't risk another long
departure to Europe or Australia or even New
York.

On the other hand the American Shakespeare Festival at Stratford Connecticut looked
ideal: the money was terrible (three hundred
and fifty dollars a week) but its short summer

Shakespearian summers at Stratford Connecticut:
Ado About Nothing (with Lois Nettleton), *Antony*
Cleopatra (with Robert Ryan) and a Viola in *Twe*
Night of which Walter Kerr wrote: 'Miss Hepburn
always been one of the most fetching creatures to h
been bestowed on our time, and fetching isn't the h
it as the lady takes a stubborn, or a petulant, or ev
slightly fearful stance in her white ducks, brass bot
jacket and sleek black boater.' *New York Times*

138

seasons compared very favourably with the time it would take to get a new production through a tour and onto Broadway and what was more Stratford, like the Old Vic, was offering a range of good roles in repertoire: in the '57 season there Kate played Portia to Morris Carnovsky's Shylock and Beatrice to Alfred Drake's Benedick in *Much Ado About Nothing*, and three seasons later she went back to play Cleopatra to Robert Ryan's Antony and Viola in *Twelfth Night* – these last two at the age of fifty-one.

Reviews for all of these final Shakespearian outings were always mixed (not least for John Houseman's *Much Ado About Nothing* which he gave a Texan-Mexican setting) but Kate loved the life of Stratford Connecticut: close to home, it also reminded her of her early summers in stock and this particular Stratford, lacking either the intensity or the critical distinction of the ones in Warwickshire and Ontario, had a kind of backwoods rough-and-readiness which had always appealed to her.

In the three years that separated those two seasons, Hepburn settled into a kind of semi-retirement with Tracy: both had decided that they were already old enough and rich enough not to have to work unless something really strong came along, and both began to feel that having over almost twenty years now established strong reputations it would be a pity to let them drift away into the kind of pensionable rubbish that a lot of their contemporaries were allowing themselves to do. They had no children to worry about, no large houses to support, no tomorrows that couldn't be left to take care of themselves. And besides, Spencer Tracy was not a well man.

*'I'm a star . . . it's all I
know how to be'*

11

YEARS AGO, ROBERT BENCHLEY HAD ONCE SAID OF Hepburn that 'though not a great actress, she has a certain distinction which with training might possibly take the place of great acting in an emergency' and now it seemed that these emergencies were starting to come thick and fast. In 1959, with Tracy back on his feet and in the business and beginning to think about *Inherit the Wind*, Kate decided that it was safe again to leave him for a while. What took her in that year to London for three months (and a hundred and seventy-five thousand dollars) was a darkly intriguing project – the filming of Tennessee Williams's everyday story of homo-sexuality and madness and cannibalism in the Deep South, *Suddenly Last Summer*.

This had started out off-Broadway a year earlier as half of a double-bill called *The Garden District*, and a lot of talent was now involved in bringing it to the screen. Gore Vidal had done the screenplay with Williams himself, Sam Spiegel was the producer, Joseph Mankiewicz the director and Elizabeth Taylor was to be the girl whom Hepburn tries to get lobotomised by Montgomery Clift so that she will not recall the details of how her cousin (Hepburn's son) got unfortunately eaten to death on a North African beach by the boys he was attempting to seduce.

In the dragon-mother Mrs Venable (whose first entrance is descending in a private elevator demanding of the doctor 'Are you interested in the Byzantine?') Hepburn had rightly recognised one of the great gothic creations of even Williams's fevered imagination, and she gave a larger-than-life dowager performance of tremendous strength and courage. But this was a far from happy set. Taylor was sulking over the hostile British press reaction to her Eddie Fisher marriage, Clift was deeply addicted to a wide range of drugs, and Kate was as always worried about Tracy back in California. The mood was not eased when Mankiewicz tried to fire the unreliable Clift and Hepburn simultaneously discovered that they were shooting her in the most unflattering possible light. Though she had happily worked with both producer and director before (Spiegel on *The African Queen*, Mankiewicz on *The Philadelphia Story*) she finished *Suddenly Last Summer* by spitting at them both in the eye, on the grounds that they had treated their cast less than courteously through a difficult time.

But for all its unhappiness of shooting and over-the-top theatricality of style, *Suddenly Last Summer* turned out a lot better than many of Kate's recent and 'happier' films, and there are many of us who believe that the only reason neither she nor Taylor got the Oscar for it was that they were nominated in competition with each other and the voters chose to make some altogether other choice. Williams was initially nervous that Hepburn would at fifty be rather too young for the role, but concluded after seeing some early rushes that she was in fact 'brilliant'; most critics concurred that she blended overpowering mother-love, decadence and insanity into a shattering experience, and there can be no doubt that this was the film that led Hepburn into her final phase as an actress of either tragic or resilient dowagers.

It was also the film which led moviegoers into the more permissive sixties, when darker and more sexually explicit scripts were to replace the 'family entertainment' to which Hepburn's career had thus far been directed. But having sailed home on one of the first breakers of that new wave, she herself then began to be more and more selective about what she would do for either stage or screen: she did not much care for the dawn of this bleak new era in stage and cine-reality.

Back then to Shakespeare at Stratford Connecticut for the second (and last) season, and then home to Tracy and the increased amount of guarding and nursing he now needed. She didn't work again until the autumn of 1961, when she suddenly had a phone call from a neophyte producer called Ely Landau: 'I told her that I was going into motion picture pro-

'To my mind *Suddenly Last Summer*' (Hepburn here as the devouring mother, with Montgomery Clift as the pained and puzzled doctor trying to solve the mystery of why Sebastian got eaten by young men on a North African beach) 'is a decadent piece of work, sensational, barbarous and ridiculous. I loathe this film.'
C. A. Lejeune

duction and that I'd like her to do a picture for me, *Long Day's Journey Into Night*. She asked who was doing the screenplay. I told her Eugene O'Neill had done a script that was good enough for me. That seemed to please her, and then I told her I was starting to shoot in a month. She told me I was nuts, but we did start in a month and with her.'

Originally Landau had hoped Tracy might consent to play James Tyrone, but when Spencer discovered that the salary was only twenty-five thousand dollars and they were going to make it in the Bronx in five weeks flat he decided that this was perhaps not going to be quite the class of production to which he had become accustomed, and gracefully declined a role which went then to Sir Ralph Richardson. *Long Day's Journey* wound up looking, not surprisingly, very much more like a photographed play than a film, but with wonderful casting, (Hepburn, Richardson, Dean Stockwell and Jason Robards) and the intensity of Sidney Lumet's direction it remains a marvellously faithful

record of classic text – albeit an hour shorter than the 300-minute original. For Hepburn, it was at last the chance to work in O'Neill which she had first sought fifteen years earlier when she had gone to Louis B. Mayer asking to be allowed to do *Mourning Becomes Electra* with Garbo and he had told her that it was far too shocking. Now, she said: 'I no longer give a damn what people think: I don't care about clothes or possessions or anything except making the films that I want to make even if the money is terrible. I suppose you might say that neither O'Neill nor Tennessee Williams are exactly happy little fellows, but it's always happy people like me who are called on to play the unhappy ones. I come from a generation in which happy people were much more common. My parents went to Europe on their honeymoon and on the boat going over my mother began unveiling her deepest views of life and my father asked her kindly to stop. "Aren't you interested in my innermost thoughts?" she asked. "Not if those are your most innermost

'I have never been an addict of Katharine Hepburn: she strikes me usually as mannered, to say the least. But in *Long Day's Journey Into Night*, stimulated by O'Neill and Ralph Richardson, she emerges as a superb tragedienne.' *Dwight Macdonald*

thoughts," he said and they lived happily ever afterwards. Nowadays everybody seems to unburden themselves to everybody else, which is fine for us actors but very expensive for the public when they have to pay for psychiatry. These days people think they have a God-given right to do any damn thing they like and still find delicious happiness: O'Neill is saying you have to believe in something first. Even then, that may not be enough to see you through.'

For five years, after that *Long Day's Journey Into Night*, Hepburn chose not to work at all: there were rumours of all kinds of projects including even a Cukor musical but in private truth with both her father and Tracy now visibly dying, one of old age and the other of pulmonary edema, she had better things to do than think about making more movies. But then her father died and Tracy, eager to go out working rather than brooding, agreed to one final Stanley Kramer picture. This, written by William Rose who had also scripted the last Kramer-Tracy picture, *It's A Mad Mad Mad World*, was to be a family affair for Hepburn. *Guess Who's Coming To Dinner?* while conceived in many ways as Tracy's own farewell to the screen, was also to be an introduction to it for Kate's niece Katharine Houghton playing their white daughter who gets engaged to a black doctor (Sidney Poitier). Hepburn here took third billing to Tracy and Poitier, and agreed that in return for considerable press and studio co-operation during the actual shooting, she would sacrifice her usually obsessive demands for privacy and give at least one major press conference to introduce her niece. Few apart from the immediate family and Kramer knew precisely how close Tracy was to death, and fewer still knew that Hepburn had agreed to put up her own salary as insurance for the film when it was realised that no more usual insurance company would touch it in the light of Tracy's health. Twelve years later, and on another Hepburn picture, that was a gesture that was to be repeated by Jane Fonda when it

was realised that her own father was uninsurable for *On Golden Pond*.

Tracy in fact died just two weeks after the completion of *Guess Who's Coming to Dinner?*, thereby lending tremendous poignancy to a film that was otherwise alarmingly inclined to cop out of every single race-relation issue that it raised. Rose was a comic writer of considerable distinction (not least *Genevieve*) but here, faced with being the first writer to bring to the big-star screen the story of an inter-racial marriage in the newly liberal sixties, he loaded the dice more than somewhat by making Poitier not just black but a Nobel-candidate Rhodes Scholar who was also a consultant to the United Nations. There were therefore those of us in the audience who wondered whether even Kate's equally patrician Wasp niece was actually good enough for him, though this did not seem to be the issue at stake here.

The great final speech in which Tracy, having been won over to a black son-in-law, makes a plea for social tolerance was in fact much the same speech as the one he'd made to the jury in two earlier Kramer pictures (*Inherit the Wind* and *Judgement at Nuremberg*) but now, coming as it was from the very brink of the grave, his whole performance seemed to be an object lesson to the future generations of actors in how these things should be done best.

Guess Who's Coming to Dinner? was, in its 1930s sets and attitudes, also of course a nostalgic farewell to one of the most enduring screen teams of all time: in their ninth and last film together, Tracy and Hepburn seemed keen to reassure audiences who had stayed with them across twenty years that they had maybe grown a little crankier and greyer with the decades but beyond that were much the same as ever. They had survived, and survival was what Hollywood was all about. On the last day of shooting Kate made a tremendously regal speech of thanks to the cast and crew, some of whom had been driven to distraction by her usual interference with everything on the set and her usual

A great farewell to Tracy: '*Guess Who's Coming to Dinner?* is an inescapably sentimental occasion. It is the late Spencer Tracy's last movie, and he is co-incidentally co-starred in it with his partner of eight previous movies, the glorious Katharine Hepburn' (with Sidney Poitier as her prospective son-in-law). 'In the course of their long careers, Tracy and Hepburn have given us so much delight, so many fond memories, that the simple fact of their presence in the same film for one final curtain call is enough to bring a lump to your throat. They bicker fondly together in their patented manner, and for me, at least, their performances in this movie are beyond the reach of criticism.' *Richard Schickel*

'It's 1183 and we're Barbarians': 'Katharine Hepburn and Peter O'Toole, leaping at one another's throats with crocodile tears in their eyes, make *Lion in Winter* a medieval variant on *The Little Foxes*. This may indeed be the performance of her entire career. Playing the relentlessly intelligent, ambitious, cunning, devious and yet after all (when one least expects it) human and vulnerable Eleanor of Aquitaine, she finds possibilities both in herself and the text which we would hardly have guessed at ... this is a monument to Katharine Hepburn as a growing, developing and still surprising actress – not merely a monument to a monument.'
John Russell Taylor

determination not to get her neck photographed even if this meant several scenes on the couch.

Two weeks later, she paid her usual morning call on Tracy and found him slumped over the kitchen table in front of a glass of milk: out of deference to the still-living Mrs Tracy, it was solemnly announced to the press that he had been found by 'a housekeeper' though on reflection that was perhaps not a bad description of the role Kate had taken on herself these past five years.

But now, she had to get back to being Great Kate again: the tremendous gap left in her private and professional life by Tracy's death was one that could really only be filled by work, and in the decade after he died she was never to do less than one stage or screen production a year, moving almost overnight from being a still officially unacknowledged widow to being a dowager Queen Mother of what was left of the movie industry.

Back in the mid-sixties, Hepburn had published a lengthy and thoughtful piece in the Virginia Law Review about a human being's right to privacy, concluding that of all currently unfashionable civil rights this was perhaps the one most worth fighting for; but now, with Tracy's death, a curious change came over her. The producer Irene Mayer Selznick (Louis B. Mayer's daughter and David Selznick's ex-wife) who has been an almost-lifelong friend of Kate's, had cherished for years the intelligent (though never-realised) dream of turning her into a director and it was she who first noted the change that came over her in the late sixties: 'Kate had always ducked the press to the point of being rude. They, in turn, were hostile. But after Spence died, Kate did less battle for her privacy. She gradually opened her door and her arms wider – I imagine because there was not so much to lose, or because there was extra to give. I remember when her phone number and address were sacred. Now she doesn't mind being caught shovelling snow in front of her

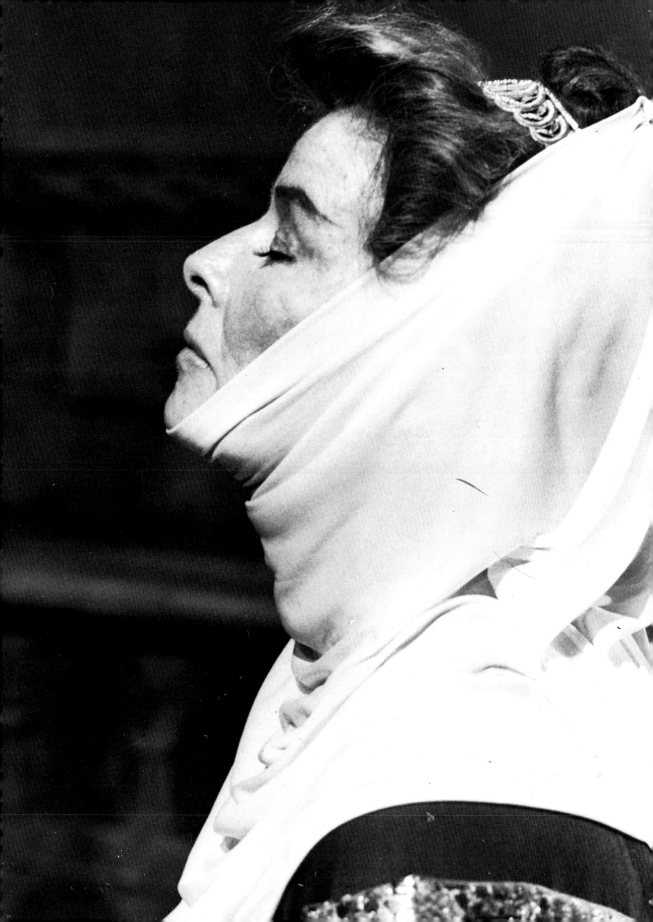

house, Not too long ago a passer-by, not up to date on the obituaries, called out "Didn't you used to be Joan Crawford?" "Not any more, I'm not" said she.'

In the year immediately following Tracy's death, Hepburn threw herself into two big movies of distinctly varying quality: the first, *The Lion in Winter*, was based on a none-too-successful stage play by James Goldman about Henry II and Eleanor of Aquitaine which conceived the epic rage of their royal-family life as a kind of medieval variant on *The Little Foxes*. Peter O'Toole was cast as Henry and took the view that Kate 'has been sent by fate to nag and torment me': nevertheless the two of them achieved a remarkable screen rapport, one for which the groundwork had been carefully prepared. The director Anthony Harvey had his entire cast rehearse (for a fortnight before shooting) in the suitably stagey surroundings of the Theatre Royal Haymarket. O'Toole had of course already played a rather younger Henry II opposite Burton's *Becket*, but now he was asked to compete with Hepburn at her most flamboyantly dramatic in a performance which John Russell Taylor reckoned was 'the best of her entire career. Playing the relentlessly intelligent, ambitious, cunning, and devious and yet after all human and vulnerable Eleanor, she finds possibilities both in herself and the text which we would hardly have guessed at.'

This film borrowed from everywhere: from *Becket*, from *Long Day's Journey*, from *A Man For All Seasons*, from *The Little Foxes*. It was pop-history but on the grand scale, never better than when Hepburn, having listened to a listing of domestic problems ranging from adultery through incest, annulment, divorce and disinheritance, shrugs 'What family doesn't have its ups and downs?'. There was a fundamental nudging vulgarity about *The Lion in Winter* which perhaps prevents it being regarded as a great film, but as Eleanor, fighting 'tusk to tusk into eternity' with Henry, Hepburn was unarguably in great dowager form.

It was now, with this enjoyable camp historical romp, that Hepburn seemed to move into the last phase of her career – one in which critics were finally to start paying often over-effusive tributes to the actress they had for so long taken for granted as half the Tracy team. Arthur Knight, for instance: 'This extraordinary woman, with her proud face and lissom figure, over the years has attacked everything from romantic frou-frou through classic tragedy to the delicious yet frequently meaningful comedies that she used to do with Spencer Tracy – and all of them gained a measure of depth and delicacy from the mere fact of her being in them. Filmgoers of the early thirties remember well the special radiance that lit up the screen whenever she appeared, no matter how dreary or unlikely the story. And when, on such occasions as *Morning Glory* or *Little Women* or *Alice Adams* she was presented with a role worthy of her talents, the incandescence of her performance became almost blinding. She has that rare but essential quality in an actress of seeming to believe in whatever she is playing so completely that her audience are compelled to believe as well.'

And Goldman's script was at least self-mocking: 'It's 1183 and we're barbarians' shrieks Hepburn with glee, and, later to a child 'Hush, dear, Mother's fighting'. But not even she could save what mother went to fight for next: an immensely starry but totally doomed film version of Giraudoux's classic play *The Madwoman of Chaillot* which was supposed to reunite her with her old mentor John Huston. Huston however quit two weeks before shooting was due to start, having quarrelled over the script, and Bryan Forbes was left to steer a tricky craft loaded with a quite remarkable number of stars: not only Hepburn but Edith Evans, Charles Boyer, Claude Dauphin, Paul Henried, Oscar Homolka, Margaret Leighton, Giulietta Masina, Nanette Newman, Richard Chamberlain, Yul Brynner, Donald Pleasence and Danny Kaye. The resultant mishmash

Hepburn, Danny Kaye, Edith Evans and the all-stars in
Bryan Forbes' 1969 *Madwoman of Chaillot*: 'Slow-
paced pic holds slim b.o. potential except for ardent
Hepburn worshippers, who will be disappointed . . .
instead of the madwoman of Chaillot she is merely an
extroverted eccentric.' *Variety*

looked like an international film festival for which somebody had forgotten to bring the film: as its own producer Ely Landau later and ruefully noted: 'We lost *Madwoman* somewhere about halfway through the production. We lost it because it was too romantic, too sentimental. A fantasy is always difficult to achieve for pictures anyway and it lacked bite'.

To mark her approval of Bryan Forbes as a Huston replacement, Hepburn gave another of her increasingly less-rare interviews, this one to a reporter who had either the impertinence or the nerve to ask if she had really loved Tracy. Kate fixed him with that most withering of all her many stares and replied simply 'Everybody loved Mr Tracy'. With Forbes (who felt at times that he had been hauled in to direct a celebrity-guest TV show rather than a film) she was however a lot gentler: 'She greeted me looking like a ravishingly attractive member of the Foreign Legion, and within the space of thirty minutes had dazzled, bewitched and flattered me into signing on for the duration of that war . . . throughout the shooting she was my keeper, nurse, masseuse, assistant director and analyst.' She also agreed to let Edith Evans stay in her villa, welcoming her with the news that she was to treat the place as her own, bearing in mind only that it was Hepburn's habit to be in bed every evening by 7.30. 'Charming' said Edith, 'and very generous. But what do people do around here if they don't wish to be in bed by half-past seven?'

Though *The Madwoman of Chaillot* proved to be a fair old disaster for all concerned ('slim box-office potential except for ardent Hepburn worshippers' thought *Variety*), during its shooting in the South of France came news that the Academy of Motion Picture Arts and Sciences had for the first time in thirty-five years seen fit to vote Hepburn an Oscar – her second, awarded for her performance in *Guess Who's Coming To Dinner?* 'And did Mr Tracy win one too?' she enquired of the housekeeper who telephoned her the news from America. On being told that he hadn't, she briskly replied that that was just fine, doubtless the Academy had meant hers to be for him too; yet again her innate sense of what was right had overcome another Hollywood goof. The Oscar clearly meant much to her: 'You know' she told Forbes, 'they don't often give it to old girls like me.'

'*Coco* is a showcase, a form of endearment, a gesture of assent, an open palm of respect. Miss Hepburn will never be old enough or tired enough to undergo one of those official evenings of tribute at which everyone gathers to summarize and reminisce. So it has been arranged right now, with her doing all the work: if *Coco* is anything, it is less a stage musical than Miss Hepburn's gala Benefit Performance and given for our benefit.' *Walter Kerr*

Kate and Coco

50c

Newsweek

...MBER 10, 1969

She was however cynically aware that there was something as ludicrous about America's new sanctification of her as there had been about her designation as 'box-office poison' back in the thirties: 'Now that I am Saint Katharine' she said, 'it is fashionable to say that I am a beauty with a well-proportioned face. But when I was beginning they thought I was just a freak with a lot of freckles. I never really bothered one way or the other, because I thought the stuff I had to work with wasn't all that bad and one or two painters seemed to quite like it. I've enjoyed my life and I've been very lucky: acting was all I ever wanted to do.'

And now she was about to test herself as an actress on the most demanding of all stages: the Broadway musical. In return for fifteen thousand dollars a week and a share of the profits, she'd agreed to play Coco Chanel in a new Alan Jay Lerner-André Previn score for which the producer Frederick Brisson had originally wanted his wife Rosalind Russell. Coco herself, however, then a formidable eighty-six, had vetoed Russell as 'too soft' but agreed that she might like to be impersonated by Hepburn whom at a brief meeting she had recognised as a kindred surviving spirit. Hepburn herself

viewed the project with undisguised terror ('I keep hoping to get knocked down by a truck on the way to rehearsal') but it had been sold to her as a challenge, and challenges were still for the taking. Coco had later admitted that she found Kate 'a little old' at sixty to be playing her eternally youthful self, but there was now a lot of expectation riding on the show. Lerner himself was still hot from *My Fair Lady* and *Camelot*, and during the early rehearsals word came that Hepburn had won her third Oscar, this time for *The Lion in Winter*, thereby making her the most honoured actress in the whole of Hollywood history.

Kate saw a lot of herself in Chanel: 'We're two females who have never been intimidated by the world, who never shifted our styles to conform to public opinion. Coco is practical, vulnerable and a fighter: she's not afraid to put herself on the chopping block and she's taken some real body blows. But her capacity for survival is what really fascinates me.'

As a casting idea, Kate as Coco was brilliant: as a musical, it was a lot less than that. For one thing, Lerner was working now not with the ailing Frederick Loewe but with a young André Previn and the score was remarkably undis-

tinguished: 'We wrote it by screaming at each other as we passed in airports,' said Previn, and the result was alas much the kind of music you get to hear in airports too. For another thing, though the show had a budget of nine hundred thousand dollars and some stunning Cecil Beaton designs, it had no actual centre: Chanel's life was told in terms of a sequence of fashion shows which looked, inevitably, just like fashion shows. Hepburn had not been on Broadway for almost twenty years, since *The Millionairess* in fact, and had never sung a professional note in her life; though she took the precaution of demanding her usual director, Michael Benthall, rehearsals were reportedly more than usually fraught (Hepburn rowed continually with the choreographer Michael Bennett) and when the show opened on 18 December 1969 there was more than one critic who thought it should simply have been called *Kate*. 'A talented flapdoodle' wrote Tom Prideaux for *Life* 'which resembles the last, lumbering capers of a bespangled dinosaur on the brink of extinction: the old-fashioned spectacular Broadway musical which, groping ever more uncertainly towards success, appears now to be an anomaly.'

Anomaly or not, Kate was capable of filling a theatre for six months regardless of reviews, a feat she was twice more to achieve over the next decade: the advance on *Coco* had been an all-time record, and huge numbers of mainly middle-class ladies from the Westchester counties formed a loyal and unshakeable hard core of supporters. When, as agreed at the end of her six-month contract, Kate left *Coco* and was replaced by the vastly better-qualified Danielle Darrieux, it closed within weeks, thereby proving that the customers had indeed come to see a show called simply *Kate*. Broadway's own opinion of what she had done was perhaps best expressed by the Tony award committee's decision that year to give their statue to Lauren Bacall (another musical newcomer) in *Applause*.

*'I'm like some weather-
beaten old monument :
people are beginning
to realise that they'll miss
me when I'm gone.'*

12

LONG BEFORE ITS BROADWAY OPENING HEPBURN had agreed to do the nationwide tour of *Coco*, and in the short break between leaving it on Broadway and starting the rehearsals for that she had also agreed (despite considerable exhaustion from the strain of singing and dancing her way through a heavy musical eight times a week) to play Hecuba in Michael Cacoyannis's film of *The Trojan Women*. August 1970 therefore found her in Spain with Vanessa Redgrave, Irene Papas and Genevieve Bujold shooting a long and tricky Euripidean script for very little money and, as it turned out, not much press acclaim either ('weak and mummified' thought Pauline Kael). Asked why she had done it, Hepburn noted 'because my time is running out, and one wants to have tried everything.'

Then it was back to a gruelling six-month tour of *Coco*, one which was not made much easier when on opening night in her own home town of Hartford a disgruntled former chauffeur leapt out of a cupboard at her and bit off the end of her finger. Kate got it sewn back on, didn't miss a performance, and saw *Coco* gracefully into its final closing: 'Well' she told the last-night audience through their cheers, 'you love me and I love you and that's about that.'

For her next film, she had planned a reunion with her beloved George Cukor on a Graham Greene script, *Travels with My Aunt*: it had never been one of his strongest tales, and a number of distinguished writers from Arthur Laurents through Jay Presson Allen to Hugh Wheeler had all tried their hands at various drafts of the screenplay. Finally Kate herself started to write it: 'for about eight months, in fact. Then George and I got the rest of it cast, had the clothes made and were all set to start shooting. Ten days before we were due in the studio I got a call from the producer saying that they weren't happy with the final draft, and were going back to one of the earlier ones. I said I wasn't happy with any of those, and they said in that case perhaps I'd like to leave the picture.'

For the first time in almost half a century she had been fired, and by MGM at that: Maggie Smith was brought in as a hasty replacement, and though both Cukor and Alec McCowen offered to resign from the picture in protest at her dismissal, Kate refused to let either of them: 'work is far too precious nowadays for it to be given away'. As the film turned out, they would have done better to make the moral gesture.

Undaunted (the word that before all others should appear on her tombstone) Hepburn came back to London to do a television film of Edward Albee's *A Delicate Balance* with Paul Scofield, Joseph Cotten and Lee Remick under the direction of Tony Richardson: ever since *Long Day's Journey Into Night* she had developed a liking for the way that classic plays could now be put quickly and economically on permanent record, and through the 1970s she was to do another three of these: Tennessee Williams's *The Glass Menagerie*, Emlyn Williams's *The Corn is Green* and a George Cukor production of *Love Among the Ruins* in which she played for the only time in her life with Laurence Olivier. After all the years of lengthy MGM production schedules, the speed of these television jobs (some of which then played limited seasons in art-house cinemas in both Britain and America) appealed to her greatly.

But acting was now something that she thought other people were taking far too seriously: 'Never forget' she told a reverent critic, 'that they don't give a Nobel Prize for it, and that Shirley Temple was doing it perfectly adequately at the age of four.' Occasionally, she admitted, she had seen greatness in acting, usually from Laurette Taylor, her great Broadway idol, or of course Tracy: 'He was elemental: air, fire, water, earth. A hugely complex man from whose tangled centre there emerged an absolute truth and simplicity of acting. As for me, I think I was just lucky enough to come along at a time when nothing like me had ever existed: there are certain dominant qualities in your own personality, and if you just play them they come over with a real zing.'

With Vanessa Redgrave in *The Trojan Women* (1971) and with Joanna Miles in *The Glass Menagerie* (1973): 'I'm a stage actress but I've always enjoyed making films, so much that I feel I should be the one who pays the producers.'

h Paul Scofield and Lee Remick in *A Delicate
nce* (1975): 'I'm a nice, simple, uncomplicated
on who likes to sweep floors and make Christmas
aths. I don't understand Albee at all.'

Bicycling through four decades of movies from *Break of Hearts* **and** *Woman of the Year* **and** *The Rainmaker* **to** *Guess Who's Coming to Dinner?* **and** *The Corn is Green*.

Ian Saynor in the Emlyn
Williams role and
Hepburn as his real-life
teacher 'Miss Moffat' in
the Cukor television film
of *The Corn is Green*
(1978): 'Oh indeed, a
wonderful part. My, I
laughed and I cried and
cried. Lovely for me. Such
a relief. A woman alive.
Not half dead.'

164

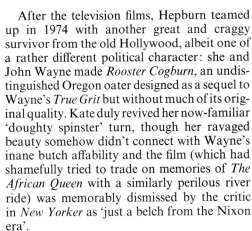

After the television films, Hepburn teamed up in 1974 with another great and craggy survivor from the old Hollywood, albeit one of a rather different political character: she and John Wayne made *Rooster Cogburn*, an undistinguished Oregon oater designed as a sequel to Wayne's *True Grit* but without much of its original quality. Kate duly revived her now-familiar 'doughty spinster' turn, though her ravaged beauty somehow didn't connect with Wayne's inane butch affability and the film (which had shamefully tried to trade on memories of *The African Queen* with a similarly perilous river ride) was memorably dismissed by the critic in *New Yorker* as 'just a belch from the Nixon era'.

But by now there was a real danger that Hepburn, like the monument she so often likened herself to, was towering above the control of any of her directors, most of whom seemed and often were young enough to be her grandsons, and was (left to herself) increasingly inclined to give way to a gritted, eccentric self-parody. Selznick, Cukor, Huston, Tracy, Philip Barry, Constance Collier, all the people who had once shaped or controlled her performances over a long career were now themselves either dead or in semi-retirement, and Kate was giving way to her over-the-top theatrical devices.

Her next play, the 1976 *A Matter of Gravity*, had been written by another mannered old dowager (Enid Bagnold) for yet a third (Edith Evans) but when it had not done well in England Bagnold had agreed to reshape it for Hepburn and Broadway.

'My career' Kate said at this time, 'has always wavered around, stumbled, fallen, picked itself up, crawled back and jumped. I'm not somebody who just sat around on a throne, but when it comes to a new script I never really listen to anybody else. As my mother always said "If you always do what interests you, then at least one person is pleased."'

165

Rooster Cogburn, **1975. Wayne on Hepburn: 'She's the best. She knows everything that's going on, understands the slightest move by anybody. I have never in my life worked with a woman who had the smell of drama as this woman has.' Left, Dick Cavett, hiding from Hepburn on one of his better TV chat shows.**

...urn has not shown up in person to collect any of ...hree recent Oscars: she was however at the 1974 ...rations to present the Irving Thalberg award to her ...riend and producer Lawrence Weingarten. Below, ... on Broadway, with an earthbound Christopher ...e, in *A Matter of Gravity* (1976).

'Here, in *On Golden Pond*, were these two immensely powerful women encircling each other like tigresses. Kate saw Jane Fonda as what she herself had been years before. Jane was concerned about Kate's authority and strength. It took time for Kate to realize that Jane actually revered her: then came trust and, after that, firm friendship.' *Mark Rydell*

And Hepburn was pleased by *A Matter of Gravity*: cured by a plastic-hip operation of the arthritis that had been troubling her for more than a year, she bounded back onto the stage as a loony matriarch in an English country house where the staff are given to levitation and her grandson (Christopher Reeve, en route to *Superman*) has brought back home a couple of homosexual friends to shock her. Essentially this was a weaker re-run of *The Chalk Garden*, Bagnold's vastly better play about English country houses in familial decay, but Hepburn made it run despite the now-usual lukewarm reviews and offstage she was getting funnier by the day: 'I have just bought a refrigerator' she told the *New York Times* in tones of outrage, 'on which the label said that the icebox made fifty-four cubes of ice every day. Yesterday I counted fifty-one, and today only forty-nine: this country is definitely in trouble.'

But even if her chosen vehicles were getting shakier and shakier in the late 1970s, critics were more and more inclined to celebrate her as cinema after cinema began to dedicate themselves to whole seasons of her lost and re-found films: as Walter Kerr put it during one such season at the Museum of Modern Art in 1976, 'Hepburn is the girl we didn't dance with, and don't we wish we had?'.

Whenever possible now, Hepburn went towards Broadway rather than Hollywood and for two very good reasons: not only was there still some sign of life in New York, whereas Los Angeles had become an unproductive desert town, but also it was there that survival worked best: you have only to consider the distinction and admiration in which Helen Hayes, Lynn Fontanne and Katharine Cornell managed to close their careers, and then compare it to the troubles that Joan Crawford, Bette Davis and Gloria Swanson had finishing theirs in style, to realise that being an old stage actress beats being an old screen actress any day.

Still, she could occasionally be tempted back, and she even began looking at her old movies now that they had started turning up on late-night television: 'I saw *Morning Glory* when I got back from the theatre the other night: made forty years ago and I should have stopped right there. I haven't learnt a thing since.' But now she really only wanted to make a film if there was something very special about it, and that didn't have to be the script. The next one she did in fact, *Olly Olly Oxen Free* (1979) had a script that could have been inscribed on the backs of envelopes by ten-year-olds and possibly was. It was so bad they couldn't even release it for three years, and when they did nobody went to see it even at drive-ins: so why had she bothered to make it? 'Because they let me play most of it up in a balloon which finally landed in the Hollywood Bowl, and how often do you get to do that at 70?'.

By the time she reached her seventieth birthday in 1979, Hepburn had worked with most if not all of the Hollywood Greats: not only Spencer Tracy but Humphrey Bogart, James Stewart, Cary Grant, John Wayne, Frederic March, John Barrymore, Charles Boyer, Burt Lancaster and Montgomery Clift. In Europe she had also worked with Laurence Olivier, Edith Evans, Peter O'Toole and she had, uniquely for an American, led the Old Vic company. There was however one legendary actor of her generation whom she had never even met until they were cast together for the film of *On Golden Pond*. The director was Mary Rydell: 'It was our first day on the set and when I heard they hadn't been introduced I was astonished; after all, together they represented a hundred years of moviemaking. So I took Kate onto the set and I said "Miss Hepburn, this is Mr Henry Fonda" and he just said "About time, too" and they started work.'

On Golden Pond was a play by Ernest Thompson which had run with moderate success off and on Broadway a couple of seasons earlier: Jane Fonda had seen in it a marvellous role in which her father could take leave of his public, much as a decade earlier Hepburn had

'If people were allowed to vote on such matters, this pair
would probably be grandparents to an entire nation,
since Fonda and Hepburn are among the very few movie
stars who have gone on working while four or five
generations have grown up.' *Richard Schickel*

seen a farewell for Tracy in *Guess Who's Coming to Dinner?* Fonda therefore acquired the screen rights, put up her own salary as insurance for her dying father, and even persuaded Hepburn to join them both in what was to be yet another great Hollywood leave-taking, the only difference being that this time Fonda, unlike Tracy, did get the valedictory Oscar and just managed to live to see it brought safely home to him.

Without that overlay of real sentiment, there is no doubt that *On Golden Pond* (billed as 'a stringent comedy' but in fact a hunk of sub-Chekhovian New England marshmallow about a couple of crusty grandparents coming to terms with their daughter and grandson and themselves) would be a very forgettable affair indeed. But because audiences came to it with a whole file of background information about the participants – the film that Jane Fonda brought as a peace-offering to the dying father she had only now begun to reconcile herself with, the film that reminded Kate of her assocation with Tracy, the film that everybody thought would never get finished because of the actors' strike and Fonda's approaching death – it became the runaway hit of the season and was generally credited with having brought middle-aged filmgoers back to the cinemas for the first time in 'star-war' years.

On Golden Pond is one of those films in which the cast spend so much of their time close to tears that it seems rude not to join them: at the end of the shooting Kate ritually presented Fonda with one of Spencer's hats, and when a few months later Hollywood presented them both with Oscars it was difficult to know whether to be more amazed that she was getting it for the fourth time or that he was only getting it for the first.

But by the time those awards were announced, Kate was already back on the boards and in another script by Ernest Thompson: this one, *The West Side Waltz*, while sharing many of *Golden Pond's* sentimental attitudes to spunky

172

The Ultimate Solution of Grace Quigley, **1983, with Nick Nolte as the killer she has hired to end her own life: 'Whatever you do, kid, always serve it up with a little dressing.'** *Spencer Tracy*

geriatrics, lacked either of the Fondas and left Kate thrashing around in a structure so fragile that you felt if she left the stage the whole set would cave in. The dialogue seemed to have been assembled from off-cuts of old Hepburn press conferences in which she gave her views on growing old with gusto, and all *The West Side Waltz* had going for it was a star who managed to keep it and herself going across a six-month tour and then a long Broadway season. But by now, as I realised watching an almost all-female audience going into a New York matinee, the play itself had become totally irrelevant and largely unheard. What those customers at the Barrymore were going to see was a personal appearance by a living legend: the fact that she happened also to be an actress had become almost incidental. Originally created out of bits of Peter Pan and Major Barbara (like many of her movie scripts), Hepburn had now become her own invention and contribution to an otherwise moribund Broadway.

After the run of *The West Side Waltz* it was announced that Kate would play Rose

Kennedy in a two-hour television movie made with the matriarch's approval: then however, in December 1982, a car she was driving near her Connecticut home skidded on a snowy road into a telegraph pole and she wound up in hospital with a badly smashed foot. To her intense irritation, most of 1983 was spent recovering from that, though by the time of her seventy-fourth birthday in November she was back in front of the cameras for her director of *The Lion in Winter*, Anthony Harvey, playing the title role in *The Ultimate Solution of Grace Quigley*, a black comedy about an old woman who, tired of life, hires a professional assassin to kill her. This was a script that Hepburn herself had commissioned from a young writer (Martin Zweiback) whom she'd met eleven years earlier with George Cukor, and whose outline had since then been turned down as too macabre by every major studio. Kate therefore, and typically, raised the money herself, made the film, and it was introduced to the world at the Cannes Festival of 1984. 'She's a legend', noted her latest co-star Nick Nolte, 'but once you get beyond that she's just a cranky old broad who can sometimes be a whole lot of fun.'

Apart from a couple of television movies (*Mrs Delafield Wants To Marry* in 1986 and *Guest Appearance* in 1987) in both of which she appeared as cranky but essentially game and lovable old broads, Hepburn was to occupy herself for the rest of the decade that led up to her own eightieth birthday in 1989 with two major projects. One was a book she had long promised to write on *The African Queen*, not exactly autobiographical, since she was still far too private and isolationist for that, but instead a blow-by-blow description of what it was like to be on an often uneasy African jungle location with Bogart and Huston at their most tempestuous.

The other project was even closer to her heart: a major television documentary about the life and career of her beloved Spencer Tracy during which she decided for the first time and albeit still very cautiously to spell out in public the precise nature of their relationship for a wide audience.

Still crackling with energy, still refusing to suffer fools gladly or most journalists at all, Hepburn spent her late seventies battling with a form of Parkinson's Disease, and fighting off demands that she write a fuller account of her remarkable life or conform to anyone's expectations of Katharine of Arrogance. Invincible and unbeatable, still possessed by a waspish wit and a New England conviction that old ladies were supposed to be feisty rather than cosily lovable, she would occasionally appear to give the minimum number of interviews needed to sell her book or the television dramas. From most of these she emerged intelligent, legendary and essentially feminist. Despite an artificial hip and a foot still painful from the car crash, she gave few signs of age or infirmity, talked increasingly of the responsibility of women of all ages to fix up a world that men seemed to have got horribly wrong, and generally behaved like the cockeyed tomboy she had always played on screen.

'What thrills me now', she told an interviewer in 1989, 'is a beautiful sunset or a deer running through a forest: making films today is all a matter of money, as great big companies want to see results. But film was and is still a romantic business, just as life is romantic – we have this enormous thing we can do with what we call ourselves'.

Grace under pressure was what Hepburn had always understood best, and as old age and an increasingly unworthy film industry began to tell on her, she simply got more graceful: 'I am canny and very resolute. It's all to do with common sense in the end. I don't see the interest in playing old ladies in wheelchairs: who will want to see that? Certainly not the old ladies in wheelchairs. One should keep as mobile as possible, but that doesn't mean I want to go on living forever. I'm not afraid to die: I think I'll just go to sleep. And dying has its virtues, not to have to take responsibility any more. Anybody with brains of my age knows that it can not be far off, but I know so many people who are scared of this and that, and I don't scare so easily'.

Asked years earlier if she ever planned a real retirement, Hepburn had said 'in a lifetime of gardening, I have never yet seen a laurel on which anyone could really rest comfortably. There are no laurels in my life, just new challenges. Nor do I really believe that age entitles one to any extra benefits. To say "Oh, isn't she marvelous for her age" is just about the most condescending remark one can think of'.

Almost exactly half a century ago, when she had finally reached the end of the tour of *The Philadelphia Story* after playing it on Broadway and the road for more than a year, Kate refused to allow the curtain to descend on its last night 'I didn't want that play ever to end, so at the closing performance, when we got to the final scene, I gave a signal to the stage manager and we all just walked off the set with the curtain still up'.

Somehow, one suspects that Hepburn still wants that curtain left up on her career; and indeed on her life itself.

FILMOGRAPHY

1 A Bill of Divorcement △
DIRECTOR George Cukor
SCENARIO Howard Estabrook & Harry Wagstaff Gribble, based on the play by Clemence Dane
PHOTOGRAPHY Sid Hickox
EDITOR Arthur Roberts
CAST Hillary Fairfield (John Barrymore); Margaret Fairfield (Billie Burke); Sydney Fairfield (Katharine Hepburn), Kit Humphrey (David Manners); Doctor Alliot (Henry Stephenson); Gray Meredith (Paul Cavanagh); Aunt Hester (Elizabeth Patterson); Bassett (Gayle Evers); Party Guest (Julie Haydon)
RUNNING TIME 67 minutes
RELEASED 1932
PRODUCED BY RKO Radio

2 Christopher Strong △
DIRECTOR Dorothy Arzner
SCENARIO Zoë Akins, based on a novel by Gilbert Frankau
PHOTOGRAPHY Bert Glennon
EDITOR Arthur Roberts
CAST Lady Cynthia Darrington (Katharine Hepburn); Sir Christopher Strong (Colin Clive); Lady Elaine Strong (Billie Burke); Monica Strong (Helen Chandler); Harry Rawlinson (Ralph Forbes); Carrie Valentin (Irene Browne); Carlo (Jack La Rue); Bryce Mercer (Desmond Roberts); Bradford, the Maid (Gwendolyn Logan); Fortune Teller (Agostino Borgato); Girl at Party (Margaret Lindsay); Mechanic (Donald Stewart); Second Maid (Zena Savina)
RUNNING TIME 77 minutes
RELEASED 1933
PRODUCED BY RKO Radio

3 Morning Glory △
DIRECTOR Lowell Sherman
SCENARIO Howard J. Green, based on the play by Zoë Akins
PHOTOGRAPHY Bert Glennon
EDITOR George Nicholls Jr
CAST Eva Lovelace (Katharine Hepburn); Joseph Sheridan (Douglas Fairbanks Jr); Louis Easton (Adolphe Menjou); Rita Vernon (Mary Duncan); Robert Harley Hedges (C. Aubrey Smith); Pepe Velez, the Gigolo (Don Alvarado); Will Seymour (Fred Santley); Henry Lawrence (Richard Carle); Charles Van Dusen (Tyler Brooke); Gwendolyn Hall (Geneva Mitchell); Nellie Navare (Helen Ware); Maid (Theresa Harris)
RUNNING TIME 74 minutes
RELEASED 1933
PRODUCED BY RKO Radio

4 Little Women △
DIRECTOR George Cukor
SCENARIO Sarah Y. Mason, Victor Heerman, based on the novel by Louisa May Alcott
PHOTOGRAPHY Henry Gerrard
EDITOR Jack Kitchin
CAST Jo (Katharine Hepburn); Amy (Joan Bennett); Professor Bhaer (Paul Lukas); Aunt March (Edna May Oliver); Beth (Jean Parker); Meg (Frances Dee); Mr Laurence (Henry Stephenson); Laurie (Douglass Montgomery); Brooke (John Davis Lodge); Marmee (Spring Byington); Mr March (Samuel S. Hinds); Hannah (Mabel Colcord); Mrs Kirke (Marion Ballou); Mamie (Nydia Westman); Dr Bangs (Harry Beresford); Flo King (Marina Schubert); Girls at the Boarding House (Dorothy Gray, June Filmer); Mr Davis (Olin Howland)
RUNNING TIME 113 minutes
RELEASED 1933
PRODUCED BY RKO Radio

5 Spitfire △

DIRECTOR John Cromwell
SCENARIO Jane Murfin, Lula Vollmer, based on the play *Trigger* by Lula Vollmer
PHOTOGRAPHY Edward Cronjager
EDITOR William H. Morgan
CAST Trigger Hicks (Katharine Hepburn); J. Stafford (Robert Young); G. Fleetwood (Ralph Bellamy); Eleanor Stafford (Martha Sleeper); Bill Grayson (Louis Mason); Etta Dawson (Sara Haden); Granny Raines (Virginia Howell); Mr Sawyer (Sidney Toler); West Fry (High Ghere); Mrs Sawyer (Therese Wittler); Jake Hawkins (John Beck)
RUNNING TIME 86 minutes
RELEASED 1934
PRODUCED BY RKO Radio

on the play by Sir James M. Barrie
PHOTOGRAPHY Henry Gerrard
EDITOR William Hamilton
CAST Babbie (Katharine Hepburn); Gavin (John Beal); Doctor McQueen (Donald Crisp); Thammas (Lumsden Hare); Wearyworld (Andy Clare); Margaret (Beryl Mercer); Micah Dow (Billy Watson); Jean (Dorothy Stickney); Nanny (Mary Gordon); Lord Rintoul (Frank Conroy); Evalina (Eily Malyon); Captain Halliwell (Reginald Denny); Munn (Leonard Carey); Carfrae (Herbert Bunsdon); John Spens (Harry Beresford); Sneck (Barlow Borland); Maid (May Beatty)
RUNNING TIME 110 minutes
RELEASED 1934
PRODUCED BY RKO Radio

7 Break of Hearts ◁

DIRECTOR Philip Moeller
SCENARIO Sarah Y. Mason, Victor Heerman, Anthony Veiller, based on a story by Lester Cohen
PHOTOGRAPHY Robert De Grasse
EDITOR William Hamilton
CAST Constance Dane (Katharine Hepburn); Franz Roberti (Charles Boyer); Johnny Lawrence (John Beal); Professor Talma (Jean Hersholt); Marx (Sam Hardy); Miss Wilson (Inez Courtney); Sylvia (Helene Millard); Pazzini (Ferdinand Gottschalk); Elise (Susan Fleming); Schubert (Lee Kohlmar); Didi Smith-Lennox (Jean Howard); Phyllis (Anne Grey); plus Jason Robards Sr. in a bit part
RUNNING TIME 78 minutes
RELEASED 1935
PRODUCED BY RKO Radio

8 Alice Adams ▽

DIRECTOR George Stevens
SCENARIO Dorothy Yost, Mortimer Offner, based on the novel by Booth Tarkington
PHOTOGRAPHY Robert De Grasse
EDITOR Jane Loring
CAST Alice Adams (Katharine Hepburn); Arthur Russell (Fred MacMurray); Mr Adams (Fred Stone); Mildred Palmer (Evelyn Venable); Walter Adams (Frank Albertson); Mrs Adams (Ann Shoemaker); Mr Lamb (Charles Grapewin); Frank Dowling (Grady Sutton); Mrs Palmer (Hedda Hopper); Mr Palmer (Jonathan Hale); Henrietta Lamb (Janet McLeod); Mrs Dowling (Virginia Howell); Mrs Dresser (Zeffie Tilbury); Ella Dowling (Ella McKenzie); Malena (Hattie McDaniel)
RUNNING TIME 100 minutes
RELEASED 1935
PRODUCED BY RKO Radio

6 The Little Minister △

DIRECTOR Richard Wallace
SCENARIO Jane Murfin, Sarah Y. Mason and Victor Heerman (additional scenes by Mortimer Offner and Jack Wagner) based

(Brandon Hurst); Lexington (Wilfred Lucas); Kirkcaldy (D'Arcy Corrigan); Douglas (Frank Baker); Faudoncide (Cyril McLaglen); English Fisherman (Lionel Belmore); His Wife (Doris Lloyd); His Son (Bobby Watson); Sir Francis Knellys (Robert Warwick); Judges (Ivan Simpson, Murray Kinnell, Lawrence Grant, Nigel De Brulier, Barlowe Borland); Sir Francis Walsingham (Walter Byron); Sergeant (Wyndham Standing); Duke of Kent (Earle Foxe); Du Croche (Paul McAllister); Chatelard (Gaston Glass); Nobleman (Neil Fitzgerald); Prince James (Jean Kircher and Judith Kircher)
RUNNING TIME 123 minutes
RELEASED 1936
PRODUCED BY RKO Radio

Marshall); Flora Thistlewaite (Elizabeth Allan); Judge Thistlewaite (Donald Crisp); Young Flora (Doris Dudley); Alan (David Manners); Betty Bumble (Lucile Watson); Gerald (Van Heflin); Piper (Eily Malyon); Aunt Serena (Margaret Seddon); Young Girl (Molly Lamont); Mr White (Lionel Pape); Lady Gaythorne (Constance Lupino); Lady Rinlake (Lillian Kemble-Cooper); Signor Grassi (Nick Thompson); Signora Grassi (Inez Palange); Hallan Boy (Tony Romero); Italian Bit (Joe Mack); Flora, Age 10 (Marilyn Knowlden); Flora, Age 5 (Bonnie June McNamara); Flora, as Infant (Marilyn French)
RUNNING TIME 88 minutes
RELEASED 1936
PRODUCED BY RKO Radio

9 Sylvia Scarlett △
DIRECTOR George Cukor
SCENARIO Gladys Unger, John Collier, Mortimer Offner, based on the novel *The Early Life and Adventures of Sylvia Scarlett* by Compton MacKenzie
PHOTOGRAPHY Joseph August
EDITOR Jane Loring
CAST Sylvia Scarlett (Katharine Hepburn); Jimmy Monkley (Cary Grant); Michael Fane (Brian Aherne); Henry Scarlett (Edmund Gwenn); Lily (Natalie Paley); Maudie Tilt (Dennie Moore); Drunk (Lennox Pawle); Bobby (Harold Cheevers); Sergeant Major (Lionel Pape); Turnkey (Robert [Bob] Adair); Stewards (Peter Hobbes, Leonard Mudie, Jack Vanair); Conductor (Harold Entwhistle); Stewardess (Adrienne D'Ambricourt); Pursers (Gaston Glass, Michael S. Visaroff); Maid (Bunny Beatty); Customs Inspectors (E. E. Clive, Edward Cooper, Olaf Hytten); Russian (Dina Smirnova); Frenchman (George Nardelli)
94 minutes
RELEASED 1936
PRODUCED BY RKO Radio

11 A Woman Rebels ▽
DIRECTOR Mark Sandrich
SCENARIO Anthony Veiller, Ernest Vajda, based on the novel *Portrait of a Rebel* by Netta Syrett
PHOTOGRAPHY Robert De Grasse
EDITOR Jane Loring
CAST Pamela Thistlewaite (Katharine Hepburn); Thomas Lane (Herbert

10 Mary of Scotland ▷
DIRECTOR John Ford
SCENARIO Dudley Nichols, based on the play by Maxwell Anderson
PHOTOGRAPHY Joseph H. August
EDITOR Jane Loring
CAST Mary Stuart (Katharine Hepburn); Earl of Bothwell (Frederic March); Elizabeth Tudor (Florence Eldridge); Darnley (Douglas Watson); David Rizzio (John Carradine); Morton (Robert Barrat); Leicester (Gavin Muir); James Stuart Moray (Ian Keith); John Knox (Moroni Olsen); Ruthven (William Stack); Randolph (Ralph Forbes); Throckmorton (Alan Mowbray); Mary Beaton (Frieda Inescort); Huntley (Donald Crisp); Lindsay (David Torrence); Mary Livingston (Molly Lamont); Mary Fleming (Anita Colby); Mary Seton (Jean Fenwick); Burghley (Lionel Pape); Donal (Alec Craig); Nurse (Mary Gordon); Messenger (Monte Blue); Maitland (Leonard Mudie); Arian

12 Quality Street △
DIRECTOR George Stevens
SCENARIO Mortimer Offner, Allan Scott, based on the play by Sir James M. Barrie
PHOTOGRAPHY Robert De Grasse
EDITOR Henry Berman
CAST Phoebe Throssel (Katharine Hepburn); Dr Valentine Brown (Franchot Tone); Susan Throssel (Fay Bainter); Sergeant (Eric Blore); Patty (Cora Witherspoon); Mary Willoughby (Estelle Winwood); Henrietta Turnbull (Florence Lake); Fanny Willoughby (Helena Grant); Isabella (Bonita Granville); Arthur (Clifford Severn); William Smith (Sherwood Bailey); Ensign Blades (Roland Varno); Charlotte Parratt (Joan Fontaine); Lieutenant Spicer (William Bakewell); Postman (York Sherwood); Student (Carmencita Johnson)
RUNNING TIME 83 minutes
RELEASED 1937
PRODUCED BY RKO Radio

13 Stage Door △
DIRECTOR Gregory La Cava
SCENARIO Morrie Ryskind, Anthony Veiller,
based on the play by Edna Ferber, George
S. Kaufman
PHOTOGRAPHY Robert De Grasse
EDITOR William Hamilton
CAST Terry Randall (Katharine Hepburn);
Jean Maitland (Ginger Rogers); Anthony
Powell (Adolphe Menjou); Linda Shaw
(Gail Patrick); Catherine Luther
(Constance Collier); Kaye Hamilton
(Andrea Leeds); Henry Sims (Samuel S.
Hinds); Judy Canfield (Lucille Ball);
Richard Carmichael (Pierre Watkin);
Harcourt (Franklin Pangborn); Mrs Orcutt
(Elizabeth Dunne); Hattie (Phyllis
Kennedy); Butcher (Grady Sutton);
Milbank (Jack Carson); Dukenfield (Fred
Santley); Bill (William Corson); Stage
Director (Frank Reicher); Eve (Eve Arden);
Annie (Ann Miller); Ann Braddock (Jane
Rhodes); Mary (Margaret Early); Dizzy
(Jean Rouverol); Olga Brent (Norma
Drury); Susan (Peggy O'Donnell);
Madeline (Harriett Brandon); Cast of Play
(Katherine Alexander, Ralph Forbes, Mary
Forbes, Huntley Gordon); Aide (Lynton
Brent); Elsworth (Theodore Von Eltz);
Playwright (Jack Rice); Chauffeur (Harry
Strang); Baggageman (Bob Perry); Theatre
Patron (Larry Steers); Actresses (Mary
Bovard, Frances Gifford); Eve's Cat
(Whitey the Cat)
RUNNING TIME 92 minutes
RELEASED 1937
PRODUCED BY RKO Radio

14 Bringing up Baby ▷
DIRECTOR Howard Hawks
SCENARIO Dudley Nichols, Hagar Wilde,
based on a story by Hagar Wilde

PHOTOGRAPHY Russell Metty
EDITOR George Hively
CAST Susan Vance (Katharine Hepburn);
David Huxley (Cary Grant); Major Horace
Applegate (Charles Ruggles); Aunt
Elizabeth (May Robson); Constable
Slocum (Walter Catlett); Mr Gogarty
(Barry Fitzgerald); Dr Fritz Lehmann
(Fritz Feld); Mrs Gogarty [Hannah] (Leona
Roberts); Alexander Peabody (George
Irving); Mrs Lehmann (Tala Birell); Alice
Swallow (Virginia Walker); Elmer (John
Kelly); George, the Dog (Asta); Baby, the
Leopard (Nissa); Louis, the Headwaiter
(George Humbert); Joe, the Bartender
(Ernest Cossart); David's Caddy (Brooks
Benedict); Roustabout (Jack Carson);

Circus Manager (Richard Lane); Motor
Cop (Ward Bond)
RUNNING TIME 102 minutes
RELEASED 1938
PRODUCED BY RKO Radio

15 Holiday (GB titles: Free to Live/ △
Unconventional Linda)
DIRECTOR George Cukor
SCENARIO Donald Ogden Stewart, Sidney
Buchman, based on the play by Philip Barry
PHOTOGRAPHY Franz Planer
EDITOR Otto Meyer, Al Clark
CAST Linda Seton (Katharine Hepburn);
Johnny Case (Cary Grant); Julia Seton
(Doris Nolan); Ned Seton (Lew Ayres);
Nick Potter (Edward Everett Horton);

Edward Seton (Henry Kolker); Laura
Cram (Binnie Barnes); Susan Potter (Jean
Dixon); Seton Cram (Henry Daniell);
Banker (Charles Trowbridge); Henry
(George Pauncefort); Thayer (Charles
Richman); Jennings (Mitchell Harris);
Edgar (Neil Fitzgerald); Grandmother
(Marion Ballou); Man in Church (Howard
Hickman); Woman in Church (Hilda
Plowright); Cook (Mabel Colcord);
Woman on Staircase (Bess Flowers);
Scotchmen (Harry Allen, Edward Cooper);
Farmer's Wife (Margaret McWade);
Farmer (Frank Shannon); Farm Girl
(Aileen Carlyle); Taxi Driver (Matt
McHugh); Steward (Maurice Brierre); Mrs
Jennings (Esther Peck); Mrs Thayer (Lillian
West); Grandfather (Luke Cosgrave)
RUNNING TIME 95 minutes
RELEASED 1938
PRODUCED BY Columbia

16 The Philadelphia Story △
DIRECTOR George Cukor
SCENARIO Donald Ogden Stewart, based on
the play by Philip Barry
PHOTOGRAPHY Joseph Ruttenberg
EDITOR Frank Sullivan
CAST C. K Dexter (Cary Grant); Tracy Lord
(Katharine Hepburn); Mike Connor (James
Stewart); Liz Imbrie (Ruth Hussey);
George Kittredge (John Howard); Uncle
Willie (Roland Young); Seth Lord (John
Halliday); Dinah Lord (Virginia Weidler);
Margaret Lord (Mary Nash); Sidney Kidd
(Henry Daniell); Edward (Lionel Pape);
Thomas (Rex Evans); John (Russ Clark);
Librarian (Hilda Plowright); Manicurist
(Lita Chevret); Bartender (Lee Phelps);
Mac (David Clyde); Willie's Butler (Claude
King); Doctor Parsons (Robert De Bruce);
Elsie (Veda Buckland); First Mainliner
(Dorothy Fay); Second Mainliner (Florine
McKinney); Third Mainliner (Helene
Whitney); Fourth Mainliner (Hillary
Brooke)
RUNNING TIME 112 minutes
RELEASED 1940
PRODUCED BY Metro-Goldwyn-Mayer

17 Woman of the Year △
DIRECTOR George Stevens
SCENARIO Ring Lardner Jr, Michael Kanin
PHOTOGRAPHY Joseph Ruttenberg
EDITOR Frank Sullivan
CAST Sam Craig (Spencer Tracy); Tess
Harding (Katharine Hepburn); Ellen
Whitcomb (Fay Bainter); Clayton
(Reginald Owen); William Harding (Minor
Watson); Pinkie Peters (William Bendix);
Flo Peters (Gladys Blake); Gerald (Dan
Tobin); Phil Whittaker (Roscoe Karns);
Ellis (William Tannen); Dr Martin Lubbeck
(Ludwig Stossel); Matron at Refugee Home
(Sara Haden); Alona (Edith Evanson);
Chris (George Kezas); Reporter (Jimmy
Conlin); Justice of the Peace (Henry
Roquemore); Harding's Chauffeur (Cyril
Ring); Punchy (Ben Lessy); Pal (Johnny
Berkes); Reporter (Ray Teal); Football
Player (Duke York); Adolph (Edward
McWade); Building Superintendent (Joe
Yule); Chairlady (Winifred Harris); Man at
Banquet (William Holmes)
RUNNING TIME 114 minutes
RELEASED 1942
PRODUCED BY Metro-Goldwyn-Mayer

18 Keeper of the Flame ▷
DIRECTOR George Cukor
SCENARIO Donald Ogden Stewart, based on
the novel by I. A. R. Wylie
PHOTOGRAPHY William Daniels
EDITOR James E. Newcom
CAST Steven O'Malley (Spencer Tracy);
Christine Forrest (Katharine Hepburn);
Clive Kerndon (Richard Whorf); Mrs
Forrest (Margaret Wycherly); Mr
Arbuthnot (Donald Meek); Freddie Ridges
(Horace Stephen McNally); Jane Harding
(Audrey Christie); Dr Fielding (Frank
Craven); Geoffrey Midford (Forrest
Tucker); Orion (Percy Kilbride); Jason
Rickards (Howard Da Silva); Jeb Rickards
(Darryl Hickman); Piggot (William
Newell); John (Rex Evans); Anna (Blanche
Yurka); Janet (Mary McLeod); William

(Clifford Brooke); Ambassador (Craufurd
Kent); Messenger Boy (Mickey Martin);
Reporters (Manart Kippen, Donald
Gallaher, Cliff Danielson); Men (Major
Sam Harris, Art Howard, Harold Miller);
Pet (Jay Ward); Susan (Rita Quigley);
Auctioneer (Dick Elliott); Lawyer (Edward
McWade); Boy Reporter (Irvin Lee); Girls
(Diana Dill [Diana Douglas], Gloria
Tucker); Minister's Voice (Dr Charles
Frederick Lindsley); Tim (Robert Pittard);
Gardner (Louis Mason)
RUNNING TIME 100 minutes
RELEASED 1942
PRODUCED BY Metro-Goldwyn-Mayer

19 Stage Door Canteen

DIRECTOR Frank Borzage
SCENARIO Delmer Daves
PHOTOGRAPHY Harry Wild
EDITOR Hal Kern
CAST Eileen (Cheryl Walker); Ed 'Dakota' Smith (William Terry); Jean (Marjorie Riordan); 'California' (Lon McCallister); Ella Sue (Margaret Early); 'Texas' (Michael Harrison); Mamie (Dorothea Kent); 'Jersey' (Fred Brady); Lillian (Marion Shockley); The Australian (Patrick O'Moore); Girl (Ruth Roman)
And, the Stars at the Stage Door Canteen: Judith Anderson, Henry Armetta, Benny Baker, Kenny Baker, Tallulah Bankhead, Ralph Bellamy, Edgar Bergen & Charlie McCarthy, Ray Bolger, Helen Broderick, Ina Claire, Katharine Cornell, Lloyd Corrigan, Jane Cowl, Jane Darwell, William Demarest, Virginia Field, Dorothy Fields, Gracie Fields, Lynn Fontanne, Arlene Francis, Vinton Freedley, Billy Gilbert, Lucile Gleason, Vera Gordon, Virginia Grey, Helen Hayes, Katharine Hepburn, Hugh Herbert, Jean Hersholt, Sam Jaffe, Allen Jenkins, George Jessel, Roscoe Karns, Virginia Kaye, Tom Kennedy, Otto Kruger, June Lane, Betty Lawford, Gertrude Lawrence, Gypsy Rose Lee, Alfred Lunt, Bert Lytell, Harpo Marx, Aline MacMahon, Elsa Maxwell, Helen Menken, Yehudi Menuhin, Ethel Merman, Ralph Morgan, Alan Mowbray, Paul Muni, Elliott Nugent, Merle Oberon, Franklin Pangborn, Helen Parrish, Brock Pemberton, George Raft, Lanny Ross, Selena Royle, Martha Scott, Cornelia Otis Skinner, Ned Sparks, Bill Stern, Ethel Waters, Johnny Weissmuller, Arleen Whelan, Dame May Whitty, Ed Wynn
And:
Count Basie and His Band; Xavier Cugat and his Orchestra, with Lina Romay; Benny Goodman and His Orchestra, with Peggy Lee; Kay Kyser and His Band; Freddy Martin and His Orchestra; Guy Lombardo and His Orchestra
RUNNING TIME 133 minutes
RELEASED 1943
PRODUCED BY Sol Lesser Productions released through United Artists

20 Dragon Seed

DIRECTOR Jack Conway, Harold S. Bucquet
SCENARIO Marguerite Roberts, Jane Murfin, based on the novel by Pearl S. Buck
PHOTOGRAPHY Sidney Wagner
EDITOR Harold F. Kress
CAST Jade (Katharine Hepburn); Ling Tan (Walter Huston); Mrs Ling Tan (Aline MacMahon); Wu Lien (Akim Tamiroff); Lao Er (Turhan Bey); Lao San (Hurd Hatfield); Orchid (Frances Rafferty); Third Cousin's Wife (Agnes Moorhead); Third Cousin (Henry Travers); Captain Sato (Robert Lewis); Japanese Kitchen Overseer (J. Carrol Naish); Lao Ta (Robert Bice); Mrs Wu Lien (Jacqueline De Wit); Fourth Cousin (Clarence Lung); Neighbor Shen (Paul E. Burns); Wu Sao (Anna Demetrio); Major Yohagi (Ted Hecht); Captain Yasuda (Abner Biberman); Old Peddler (Leonard Mudie); Japanese Diplomat (Charles Lung); Student (Benson Fong); Japanese Guard (Philip Van Zandt); Japanese Officer (Al Hill); Japanese Soldier (J Alex Havier); Leader of City People (Philip Ahn); Speaker with Movies (Roland Got); Young Farmer (Robert Lee); Old Clerk (Frank Puglia); Hysterical Woman (Claire Du Brey); Innkeeper (Lee Tung Foo); Japanese Soldier (Jay Novello); Japanese Official (Leonard Strong); Narrator (Lionel Barrymore)
RUNNING TIME 147 minutes
RELEASED 1944
PRODUCED BY Metro-Goldwyn-Mayer

21 Without Love ▽

DIRECTOR Harold S. Bucquet
SCENARIO Donald Ogden Stewart based on the play by Philip Barry
PHOTOGRAPHY Karl Freund
EDITOR Frank Sullivan
CAST Pat Jamieson (Spencer Tracy); Jamie Rowan (Katharine Hepburn); Kitty Trimble (Lucille Ball); Quentin Ladd (Keenan Wynn); Paul Carrell (Carl Esmond); Edwina Collins (Patricia Morison); Professor Grinza (Felix Bressart); Anna (Emily Massey); Flower Girl (Gloria Grahame); Caretaker (George Davis); Elevator Boy (George Chandler); Sergeant (Clancy Cooper); Professor Thompson (Wallis Clark); Professor Ellis (Donald Curtis); Colonel Braden (Charles Arnt); Driver (Eddie Acuff); Porter (Clarence Muse); Headwaiter (Franco Corsaro); Pageboy (Ralph Brooks); Doctor (William Forrest); Soldiers (Garry Owen, Joe Devlin, William Newell); Sergeant (James Flavin); Girl on Elevator (Hazel Brooks)
RUNNING TIME 110 minutes
RELEASED 1945
PRODUCED BY Metro-Goldwyn-Mayer

22 Undercurrent ▷

DIRECTOR Vincente Minnelli
SCENARIO Edward Chodorov, based on a story by Thelma Strabel
PHOTOGRAPHY Karl Freund
EDITOR Ferris Webster
CAST Ann Hamilton (Katharine Hepburn); Alan Garroway (Robert Taylor); Michael Garroway (Robert Mitchum); Professor 'Dink' Hamilton (Edmund Gwenn); Lucy (Marjorie Main); Sylvia Lea Burton (Jayne Meadows); Mr Warmsley (Clinton Sundberg); Professor Joseph Bangs (Dan Tobin); Mrs Foster (Kathryn Card); George (Leigh Whipper); Justice Putnam (Charles Trowbridge); Henry Gilson (James Westerfield); Uncle Ben (Billy McLain); Julia Donnegan (Bess Flowers); Cora (Sarah Edwards); Saleslady (Betty Blythe)
RUNNING TIME 116 minutes
RELEASED 1946
PRODUCED BY Metro-Goldwyn-Mayer

24 Song of Love ▽
DIRECTOR Clarence Brown
SCENARIO Ivan Tors, Irmgard Von Cube, Allen Vincent, Robert Ardrey, based on the play by Bernard Schubert, Mario Silva
PHOTOGRAPHY Harry Stradling
EDITOR Robert J. Kern
CAST Clara Wieck Schumann (Katharine Hepburn); Robert Schumann (Paul Henreid); Johannes Brahms (Robert Walker); Franz Liszt (Henry Daniell); Professor Wieck (Leo G. Carroll); Bertha (Else Janssen); Julie (Gigi Perreau); Felix ('Tinker' Furlong); Marie (Ann Carter); Eugenie (Janine Perreau); Ludwig (Jimmie Hunt); Ferdinand (Anthony Sydes); Elsie (Eilene Janssen); Doctor Hoffman (Roman Bohmen); Haslinger (Ludwig Stossel); Princess Valerie Hohenfels (Tala Birell); Judge (Kurt Katch); King Albert (Henry Stephenson); Reinecke (Konstantin Shayne); Court Officer (Byron Foulger); Lady in Box (Josephine Whittell)
RUNNING TIME 118 minutes
RELEASED 1947
PRODUCED BY Metro-Goldwyn-Mayer

23 Sea of Grass ▽
DIRECTOR Elia Kazan
SCENARIO Marguerite Roberts, Vincent Lawrence, based on the novel by Conrad Richter
PHOTOGRAPHY Harry Stradling
EDITOR Robert J. Kern
CAST Lutie Cameron (Katharine Hepburn); Colonel James Brewton (Spencer Tracy); Brice Chamberlain (Melvyn Douglas); Sara Beth Brewton (Phyllis Thaxter); Brock Brewton (Robert Walker); Jeff (Edgar Buchanan); Doc Reid (Harry Carey); Selena Hall (Ruth Nelson); Banty (William 'Bill' Phillips); Sam Hall (James Bell); Judge White (Robert Barrat); George Cameron (Charles Trowbridge); Major Harney (Russell Hicks); Floyd McCurtin (Robert Armstrong); Andy Boggs (Trevor Bardette); Crane (Morris Ankrum); Nurse (Nora Cecil)
RUNNING TIME 123 minutes
RELEASED 1947
PRODUCED BY Metro-Goldwyn-Mayer

25 State of the Union (GB title: The World ▷ **and his Wife)**
DIRECTOR Frank Capra
SCENARIO Anthony Veiller, Myles Connolly, based on the play by Howard Lindsay, Russel Crouse
PHOTOGRAPHY George J. Folsey
EDITOR William Hornbeck
CAST Grant Matthews (Spencer Tracy); Mary Matthews (Katharine Hepburn); Spike McManus (Van Johnson); Kay Thorndyke (Angela Lansbury); Jim Conover (Adolphe Menjou); Sam Thorndyke (Lewis Stone); Lulubelle Alexander (Maidel Turner); Judge Alexander (Raymond Walburn); Bill Hardy (Charles Dingle); Grace Orval Draper (Florence Auer); Senator Lauterback (Pierre Watkin); Norah (Margaret Hamilton); Buck (Irving Bacon); Joyce (Patti Brady); Grant Jr (George Nokes);

Bellboy (Carl Switzer); Barber (Tom Pedi); Waiter (Tom Fadden); Blink Moran (Charles Lane); Leith (Art Baker); Jenny (Rhea Mitchell); First Reporter (Arthur O'Connell); Blonde Girl (Marion Martin); Wrestler (Tor Johnson); Pilot (Dave Willock); Senator (Stanley Andrews); Politician (Russell Meeker); Joe Crandall (Frank L. Clarke); Rusty Miller (David Clarke); Broder (Dell Henderson); Bradbury (Edwin Cooper); Crump (Davison Clark); Josephs (Francis Pierlot); Editor (Brandon Beach)
RUNNING TIME 122 minutes
RELEASED 1948
PRODUCED BY Liberty Film Production/ Metro-Goldwyn-Mayer

26 Adam's Rib △
DIRECTOR George Cukor
SCENARIO Garson Kanin, Ruth Gordon, based on an original story by Garson Kanin, Ruth Gordon
PHOTOGRAPHY George J. Folsey
EDITOR George Boemler
CAST Adam Banner (Spencer Tracy); Amanda Banner (Katharine Hepburn); Doris Attinger (Judy Holliday); Warren Attinger (Tom Ewell); Kip Lurie (David Wayne); Beryl Caighn (Jean Hagan); Olympia La Pere (Hope Emerson); Grace (Eve March); Judge Reiser (Clarence

Kolb); Jules Frikke (Emerson Treacy); Mrs McGrath (Polly Moran); Judge Marcasson (Will Wright); Dr Margaret Brodeigh (Elizabeth Flournoy); Mary, the Maid (Janna Da Loos); Dave (James Nolan); Roy (David Clarke); Court Clerk (John Maxwell Sholes); Court Stenographer (Marvin Kaplan); Police Matron (Gracille La Vinder); Benjamin Klausner (William Self); Emerald (Paula Raymond); Photographer (Ray Walker); Reporter (Tommy Noonan); Adam's Assistants (De Forrest Lawrence, John Fell); Amanda's Assistant (Sid Dubin); Mr Bonner (Joe Bernard); Mrs Bonner (Madge Blake); Mrs Marcasson (Marjorie Wood); Judge Poynter (Lester Luther); Mrs Poynter (Anna Q. Nilsson); Hurlock (Roger David); Elderly Elevator Operator (Louis Mason); Fat Man (Rex Evans); Young District Attoney (Charles Bastin); Subway Rider (E. Bradley Coleman)
RUNNING TIME 101 minutes
RELEASED 1949
PRODUCED BY Metro-Goldwyn-Mayer

27 The African Queen △
DIRECTOR John Huston
SCENARIO James Agee, John Huston, based on the novel by C. S. Forester
PHOTOGRAPHY Jack Cardiff
EDITOR Ralph Kemplen
CAST Charlie Allnut (Humphrey Bogart); Rose Sayer (Katharine Hepburn); Reverend Samuel Sayer (Robert Morley); Captain of Louisa (Peter Bull); First Officer (Theodore Bikel); Second Officer (Walter Gotell); Petty Officer (Gerald Onn); First Officer of Shona (Peter Swanick); Second Officer of Shona (Richard Marner)
RUNNING TIME 103 minutes
RELEASED 1951
PRODUCED BY Horizon Romulus Production/United Artists (in Technicolour)

28 Pat and Mike △
DIRECTOR George Cukor
SCENARIO Ruth Gordon, Garson Kanin, based on an original story by Ruth Gordon, Garson Kanin
PHOTOGRAPHY William Daniels
EDITOR George Boemler
CAST Mike Conovan (Spencer Tracy); Pat Pemberton (Katharine Hepburn); Davie Hucko (Aldo Ray); Collier Weld (William Ching); Barney Grau (Sammy White); Spec Cauley (George Mathews); Mr Beminger (Loring Smith); Mrs Beminger (Phyllis Povah); Hank Tasling (Charles Buchinski [Bronson]); Sam Garsell (Frank Richards); Charles Barry (Jim Backus); Police Captain (Chuck Connors); Gibby (Joseph E. Bernard); Harry MacWade (Owen McGiveney); Waiter (Lou Lubin); Bus Boy (Carl Switzer); Pat's Caddy (William Self); Caddies (Billy McLean, Frankie Darro, Paul Brinegar, 'Tiny' Jimmie Kelly); Women Golfers (Mae Clarke, Helen Eby-Rock, Elizabeth Holmes); Commentator (Hank Weaver); Sportscaster (Tom Harmon); Line Judge, Tennis Court (Charlie Murray); Themselves (Gussie Moran, Babe Didrikson Zaharias, Don Budge, Alice Marble, Frank Parker, Betty Hicks, Beverly Hanson, Helen Dettweiler)
RUNNING TIME 95 minutes
RELEASED 1952
PRODUCED BY Metro-Goldwyn-Mayer

29 Summertime (GB title: Summer Madness)
DIRECTOR David Lean
SCENARIO David Lean, H. E. Bates, based on the play The Time of the Cuckoo by Arthur Laurents
PHOTOGRAPHY Jack Hildyard
EDITOR Peter Taylor
CAST Jane Hudson (Katharine Hepburn); Renato Di Rossi (Rossano Brazzi); Signora Fiorini (Isa Miranda); Eddie Yeager (Darren McGavin); Phyl Yaeger (Mari Aldon); Mrs McIlhenny (Jane Rose); Mr McIlhenny (MacDonald Parke); Mauro (Gaitano Andiero); Englishman (Andre Morell); Vito di Rossi (Jeremy Spenser); Giovanna (Virginia Simeon)
RUNNING TIME 99 minutes
RELEASED 1955
PRODUCED BY Lopert Film Production/United Artists (in Technicolor)

30 The Rainmaker ▷
DIRECTOR Joseph Anthony
SCENARIO N. Richard Nash, based on the play by N. Richard Nash
PHOTOGRAPHY Charles Lang Jr
EDITOR Warren Low
CAST Starbuck (Burt Lancaster); Lizzie Curry (Katharine Hepburn); File (Wendell Corey); Noah Curry (Lloyd Bridges); Jim Curry (Earl Holliman); H. C. Curry (Cameron Prud'Homme); Sheriff Thomas (Wallace Ford); Snookie (Yvonne Lime); Belinda (Dottie Bee Baker); Deputy (Dan White); Townsmen (Stan Jones, John Benson, James Stone, Tony Merrill, Joe Brown); Phil Mackey (Ken Becker)
RUNNING TIME 122 minutes
RELEASED 1956
PRODUCED BY Paramount

31 The Iron Petticoat ▷
DIRECTOR Ralph Thomas
SCENARIO Ben Hecht (name removed from credits at his request) based on an original story by Harry Saltzman
PHOTOGRAPHY Ernest Steward
EDITOR Frederick Wilson
CAST Chuck Lockwood (Bob Hope); Vinka Kovelenko (Katharine Hepburn); Colonel Sklarnoff (James Robertson Justice); Ivan Kropotkin (Robert Helpmann); Dubratz (David Kossoff); Colonel Tarbell (Alan Gifford); Lewis (Paul Carpenter); Connie (Noelle Middleton); Tony Mallard (Nicholas Phipps); Paul (Sidney James); Senator (Alexander Gauge); Maria (Doris Goddard); Sutsiyawa (Tutte Lemkow); Tityana (Sandra Dorne); Lingerie Clerk (Richard Wattis); Sklarnoff's Secretary (Maria Antippas); Grisha (Martin Boddey)
RUNNING TIME 89 minutes
RELEASED 1956
PRODUCED BY Benhar Production/Metro-Goldwyn-Mayer (in Vista Vision and Technicolor)

32 Desk Set (GB title: His Other Woman) ▷
DIRECTOR Walter Lang
SCENARIO Phoebe Ephron, Henry Ephron, based on the play *The Desk Set* by William Marchant
PHOTOGRAPHY Leon Shamroy
EDITOR Robert Simpson
CAST Richard Sumner (Spencer Tracy); Bunny Watson (Katharine Hepburn); Mike Cutler (Gig Young); Peg Costello (Joan Blondell); Sylvia (Dina Merrill); Ruthie (Sue Randall); Miss Warringer (Neva Patterson); Smithers (Harry Ellerbe); Azae (Nicholas Joy); Alice (Diane Jergens); Cathy (Merry Anders); Old Lady (Ida Moore); Receptionist (Rachel Stephens); Kenny (Sammy Ogg)
RUNNING TIME 103 minutes
RELEASED 1957
PRODUCED BY Twentieth Century-Fox (in Cinemascope and colour by DeLuxe)

33 Suddenly Last Summer ▷
DIRECTOR Joseph L. Mankiewicz
SCENARIO Gore Vidal, Tennessee Williams, based on the short play by Tennessee Williams
PHOTOGRAPHY Jack Hildyard
EDITOR Thomas G. Stanford
CAST Catherine Holly (Elizabeth Taylor); Mrs Venable (Katharine Hepburn); Dr Cukrowicz (Montgomery Clift); Dr Hockstader (Albert Dekker); Mrs Holly (Mercedes McCambridge); George Holly (Gary Raymond); Miss Foxhill (Maris Villiers); Nurse Benson (Patricia Marmont); Sister Felicity (Joan Young); Lucy (Maria Britneva); Dr Hockstader's Secretary (Sheila Robbins); Young Blonde Interne (David Cameron); A Patient (Roberta Woolley)
RUNNING TIME 112 minutes
RELEASED 1959
PRODUCED BY Horizon (GB) Ltd in association with Academy Pictures and Camp Films/Columbia Pictures

34 Long Day's Journey into Night ▽
DIRECTOR Sidney Lumet
SCENARIO Eugene O'Neill, based on the play by Eugene O'Neill
PHOTOGRAPHY Boris Kaufman
EDITOR Ralph Rosenblum
CAST Mary Tyrone (Katharine Hepburn); James Tyrone Sr. (Ralph Richardson); James Tyrone Jr (Jason Robards Jr); Edmund Tyrone (Dean Stockwell); Cathleen (Jeanne Barr)
RUNNING TIME originally 174 minutes, in GB 136 minutes
RELEASED 1962
PRODUCED BY Embassy

35 Guess Who's Coming to Dinner? ▽
DIRECTOR Stanley Kramer
SCENARIO William Rose
PHOTOGRAPHY Sam Leavitt
EDITOR Robert C. Jones
CAST Matt Drayton (Spencer Tracy); John
Prentice (Sidney Poitier); Christina
Drayton (Katharine Hepburn); Joey
Drayton (Katharine Houghton);
Monsignor Ryan (Cecil Kellaway); Mr
Prentice (Roy E. Glenn Sr); Mrs Prentice
(Beah Richards); Tillie (Isabell Sandford);
Hilary St George (Virginia Christine); Car
Hop (Alexander Hay); Dorothy (Barbara
Randolph); Frankie (D'Urville Martin);
Peter (Tom Heaton); Judith (Grace
Gaynor); Delivery Boy (Skip Martin); Cab
Driver (John Hudkins)
RUNNING TIME 108 minutes
RELEASED 1967
PRODUCED BY Stanley Kramer Production/
Columbia (in Technicolor)

36 The Lion in Winter ▷
DIRECTOR Anthony Harvey
SCENARIO James Goldman, based on the
play by James Goldman
PHOTOGRAPHY Douglas Slocombe
EDITOR John Bloom
CAST Henry II (Peter O'Toole); Eleanor of
Aquitaine (Katharine Hepburn); Princess
Alais (Jane Merrow); Prince Geoffrey (John
Castle); King Philip (Timothy Dalton);
Prince Richard, the Lion-Hearted (Anthony
Hopkins); William Marshall (Nigel Stock);
Prince John (Nigel Terry), and Kenneth
Griffith, O. Z. Whitehead
RUNNING TIME 134 minutes
RELEASED 1968
PRODUCED BY Martin Poll/Avco Embassy
(in Panavision and Eastman Color)

37 The Madwoman of Chaillot ▷
DIRECTOR Bryan Forbes
SCENARIO Edward Anhalt, based on the play
by Jean Giraudoux
PHOTOGRAPHY Claud Renoir, Burnett
Guffey
EDITOR Roger Dwyre
CAST Aurelia, the Madwoman of Chaillot
(Katharine Hepburn); Broker (Charles
Boyer); Dr Jadin (Claude Dauphin);
Josephine, the Madwoman of La Concorde
(Edith Evans); Reverend (John Gavin);
General (Paul Henreid); Commissar (Oscar
Homolka); Constance, the Madwoman of
Passy (Margaret Leighton); Gabrielle, the
Madwoman of Sulpice (Giulietta Masina);
Irma (Nanette Newman); Roderick
(Richard Chamberlain); Chairman (Yul
Brynner); Prospector (Donald Pleasence);
Ragpicker (Danny Kaye); Police Sergeant
(Fernand Gravey); The Folksinger
(Gordon Heath); Julius (Gerald Sim)
RUNNING TIME 142 minutes
RELEASED 1969
PRODUCED BY Ely Landau-Bryan Forbes
Production/Commonwealth United
Corporation/Warner Bros–Seven Arts (in
Technicolor)

38 The Trojan Women ▷
DIRECTOR Michael Cacoyannis
SCENARIO Michael Cacoyannis, based on the
translation by Edith Hamilton of the play
by Euripides
PHOTOGRAPHY Alfio Contini
EDITOR Michael Cacoyannis
CAST Hecuba (Katharine Hepburn);
Andromache (Vanessa Redgrave);
Cassandra (Genevieve Bujold); Helen
(Irene Papas); Menelaus (Patrick Magee);
Talthybius (Brian Blessed); Astyanax
(Alberto Sanz); Women (Pauline Letts,
Rosaline Shanks, Pat Becket, Anna
Bentinck, Esmeralda Adam, Maria Garcia
Alonso, Nilda Alvarez, Victoria Ayllon,

Elizabeth Billencourt, Margarita Calahora,
Elena Castillo, Anna Maria Espojo, Maria
Jesus Hoyos, Conchita Leza, Margarita
Matta, Mirta Miller, Conchita Morales,
Virginia Quintana, Yvette Rees, Carmen
Segarra, Esperanza Alonso, Consolation
Alvarez, Adela Armengol, Gloria Berrogal,
Maria Borge, Carmen Cano, Renee Eber,
Katie Ellyson, Gwendoline Kocsis,
Maureen Mallall, Ivi Mavridi, Livia
Mitchell, Ersie Pittas, Catherine Rabone,
Clara Sanchiz, Laura Zarrabeitia); Singer
(Maria Farantouri)
RUNNING TIME 111 minutes
RELEASED 1972
PRODUCED BY Cinerama/Josef Shaftel (in
Eastman Color)

39 Rooster Cogburn ▷

DIRECTOR Stuart Millar
SCENARIO Martin Julien, suggested by the character Rooster Cogburn from the novel *True Grit* by Charles Portis
PHOTOGRAPHY Harry Stradling Jr
EDITOR Robert Swink
CAST Rooster Cogburn (John Wayne); Eula Goodnight (Katharine Hepburn); Breed (Anthony Zerbe); Hawk (Richard Jordan); Judge Parker (John McIntire); McCoy (Strother Martin); Luke (Paul Koslo); Red (Jack Colvin); Reverend Goodnight (Jon Lormer); Wolf (Richard Romancito); Leroy (Lane Smith); Dagby (Warren Vanders); Nose (Jerry Gatlin); Hambone (Mickey Gilbert); Jerry (Chuck Hayward); Emmett (Gary McLarty); Chen Lee (Tommy Lee)
RUNNING TIME 108 minutes
RELEASED 1975
PRODUCED BY Universal

40 Olly Olly Oxen Free (GB title: The Great Balloon Adventure)

DIRECTOR Richard A. Colla
SCENARIO Eugene Poinc, based on the story by Mario L. de Ossio, Richard Colla and Eugene Poinc
PHOTOGRAPHY Gayne Rescher
EDITOR Lee Burch
CAST Miss Pudd (Katharine Hepburn); Alby (Kevin McKenzie); Chris (Dennis Dimster); Mailman (Peter Kliman)
RUNNING TIME 83 minutes
RELEASED 1981
PRODUCED BY Sanrio

41 On Golden Pond ▽

DIRECTOR Mark Rydell
SCENARIO Ernest Thompson, based on his play
PHOTOGRAPHY Billy Williams
EDITOR Robert L. Wolfe
CAST Ethel Thayer (Katharine Hepburn); Norman Thayer Jr (Henry Fonda); Chelsea Thayer Wayne (Jane Fonda); Billy Ray (Doug McKeon); Bill Ray (Dabney Coleman); Charlie Martin (William Lanteau); Sumner Todd (Chris Rydell)
RUNNING TIME 109 minutes
RELEASED 1981
PRODUCED BY Universal

42 The Ultimate Solution of Grace Quigley

DIRECTOR Anthony Harvey
SCENARIO Martin Zweiback
PHOTOGRAPHY Larry Pizer
CAST Katharine Hepburn, Nick Nolte, Elizabeth Wilson
RELEASED 1984
PRODUCED BY Cannon/MGM/UA

TELEVISION WORK

1 A Delicate Balance ▽

DIRECTOR Tony Richardson
SCENARIO Edward Albee, based on his own play
PHOTOGRAPHY David Watkin
EDITOR John Victor Smith
CAST Agnes (Katharine Hepburn); Tobias (Paul Scofield); Julia (Lee Remick); Claire (Kate Reid); Harry (Joseph Cotten); Edna (Betsy Blair)
RUNNING TIME 134 minutes
RELEASED 1972
PRODUCED BY American Express Films (New York)/Ely Landau Organisation (London). In association with Cinevision, Montreal. For American Film Theatre.

2 The Glass Menagerie ▽

DIRECTOR Anthony Harvey
SCENARIO Tennessee Williams
EDITOR John Bloom
CAST Katharine Hepburn, Sam Waterston, Michael Moriarty, Joanna Miles
RELEASED 1973
PRODUCED BY Talent Associates/Norton Simon, Inc. Production

3 Love Among the Ruins △
DIRECTOR George Cukor
SCENARIO James Costigan
PHOTOGRAPHY Douglas Slocombe
EDITOR John Burnett, Dev Goodman
CAST Mrs Jessica Midlicott (Katharine
Hepburn); Sir Arthur Granville-Jones
(Laurence Olivier); Pratt (Leigh Lawson);
Pratt's Mother (Joan Sims); Mr Devine
(Colin Blakely)
RUNNING TIME 120 minutes
RELEASED 1975
PRODUCED BY ABC Entertainment

4 The Corn is Green ▷
DIRECTOR George Cukor
SCENARIO Ivan Davis, adapted from the play
by Emlyn Williams
EDITOR Richard Marden
CAST Miss Moffat (Katharine Hepburn);
Morgan Evans (Ian Saynor); Bessie Watty
(Toyah Willcox); Miss Ronberry (Anna
Massey); Mrs Watty (Patricia Hayes); John
Goronwy (Atro Morris); The Squire (Bill
Fraser); Sarah Pugh (Dorothea Phillips);
Idwal (Huw Richards); Robbart (Bryn
Fon); Gwyn (Dyfan Roberts); Ivor (Robin
John)
RUNNING TIME 90 minutes
RELEASED 1978
PRODUCED BY Warner Bros for CBS

Since this Filmography was compiled,
Katharine Hepburn has made no more films
but three television appearances. The first
two were in dramas: **Mrs Delafield Wants to
Marry** (1986) and **Guest Appearance** (1987).
The third was in her own documentary
about the life and career of Spencer Tracy
(1987). She also published, in 1988, her first
book: *The Making of* The African Queen, *or
How I Went To Africa With Bogart And
Bacall And Huston And Almost Lost My
Mind.*

1928

Hepburn's professional debut with the
Edwin H. Knopf Stock Company,
Baltimore, Maryland. Appeared as a Lady-
in-Waiting in *The Czarina* by Melchior
Lengyel and Lajos Biro and as a flapper in
Russell Medcraft and Norma Mitchell's *The
Cradle Snatchers.*

The Big Pond (August, New York)
by George Middleton and A. E. Thomas
DIRECTOR Edwin H. Knopf
CAST Francesco (Marius Rogati); Ronny
Davis (Reed Brown Jr.); Mrs Billings
(Marie Curtis); Mrs Livermore (Doris
Rankin); Barbara (Katharine Hepburn);
Pierre de Mirande (Kenneth MacKenna);
Henry Billings (Harlan Briggs); Sarah
(Virginia Russell); Molly Perkins (Penelope
Rowland)
PRODUCED BY Edwin H. Knopf and William
P. Farnsworth

These Days (November, New York)
by Katharine Clugston
DIRECTOR Arthur Hopkins
CAST Rosilla Dow (Mary Hall); Virginia
MacRae (Mildred McCoy); Pansy Larue
Mott (Gertrude Moran); Veronica Sims
(Katharine Hepburn); Miss Guadaloupe
Gorhan (Gladys Hopeton); 'Chippy'
Davis (Bruce Evans); Dwight Elbridge
(William Johnstone); Stephen MacRae
(Edwin Phillips); Frannie MacRae (Elaine
Koch); Mrs MacRae (May Buckley): Mr
MacRae (George MacQuarrie); Miss
Dorothea Utterback (Marie Bruce);
Stephanie Bliss (Ruth Reed); Miss Signhild
Valdemir Van Alstyne (Helen Freeman);
Miss Cleo Almeda Young (Ada Potter);
Winifred Black (Suzanne Freeman); Miss
Wilda Hall (Mary Hubbard); Miss Serena
Lash (Nellie Malcolm); Dolly (Marian
Lee); Marjory (Ruth Wilton); Richard
(Francis Corbin Burke); Guy (Willard S.
Robertson); Philip (Henri Lase); Puss
(Ruth Wilcox)
PRODUCED BY Arthur Hopkins

Holiday (November, New York)
by Philip Barry
DIRECTOR Arthur Hopkins
CAST Linda Seton (Hope Williams,
understudied by Katharine Hepburn);
Johnny Case (Ben Smith); Julia Seton
(Dorothy Tree); Ned Seton (Monroe
Owsley); Susan Potter (Barbara White);
Nick Potter (Donald Ogden Stewart);
Edward Seton (Walter Walker); Laura
Cram (Rosalie Norman); Seton Cram
(Thaddeus Clancy); Henry (Cameron
Clemens); Charles (J. Ascher Smith); Delia
(Beatrice Ames)
PRODUCED BY Arthur Hopkins

1929

Death Takes a Holiday (November, touring production)
by Alberto Casella, adapted by Walter Ferris
DIRECTOR Lawrence Marston
CAST Cora (Florence Golden); Fedele (Thomas Bate); Duke Lambert (James Dale); Alda (Ann Orr); Stephanie (Olga Birkbeck); Princess of San Luca (Viva Birkett); Baron Cesarea (Wallace Erskine); Rhoda Fenton (Lorna Lawrence); Eric Fenton (Roland Bottomley); Corrado (Martin Burton); Grazia (Katharine Hepburn); His Serene Highness, Prince Sirki, of Vitalba Alexandri (Philip Merivale); Major Whitbread (Frank Greene)
PRODUCED BY Lee Shubert

1930

A Month in the Country (March, New York)
by Ivan Turgenev, translated by M. S. Mandell
DIRECTOR Rouben Mamoulian
CAST Herr Shaaf (Charles Kraus); Anna Semenova (Minna Phillips); Natalia Petrovna (Alla Nazimova); Mikhail Aleksandrovich Rakitin (Elliot Cabot); Lizaveta Bogdanovna (Eda Heinemann); Kolia (Eddie Wragge); Alexsei Nikolaevich Bieliaev (Alexander Kirkland); Matviei (Louis Veda); Ignati Ilich Spigelski (Dudley Digges); Viera Aleksandrovna (Eunice Stoddard, understudied by Katharine Hepburn); Arkadi Sergieich Islaev (John T. Doyle); Katia (Hortense Alden, replaced by Katharine Hepburn in the second month of production); Afanasi Ivanych Bolshintsov (Henry Travers)
PRODUCED BY The Theatre Guild Inc.

Summer Stock: Katharine Hepburn appeared in G. Martinez Sierra's *A Romantic Young Lady* (translated into English by Helen and Harley Granville-Baker) and Sir James M. Barrie's *The Admirable Crichton* at the Berkshire Playhouse, Stockbridge, Massachusetts.

Art and Mrs Bottle or **The Return of the Puritan** (November, New York)
by Benn W. Levy
DIRECTOR Clifford Brooke
CAST Michael Bottle (G. P. Huntley Jr.); Judy Bottle (Katharine Hepburn); Sonia Tippet (Joyce Carey); Parlormaid (Elise Breton); George Bottle (Walter Kingsford); Celia Bottle (Jane Cowl); Charles Dawes (Lewis Martin); Max Lightly (Leon Quartermaine)
PRODUCED BY Kenneth MacGowan and Joseph Verner Reed

1931

Summer Stock: Appeared in *Just Married* by Adelaide Matthews and Anne Nichols; John Willard's *The Cat and the Canary* and *The Man Who Came Back* by Jules Eckert

Goodman, with the Ivoryton Players, Ivoryton, Connecticut.

The Animal Kingdom (September, Pittsburgh)
by Philip Barry
DIRECTOR Gilbert Miller
CAST Owen Arthur (G. Albert Smith); Rufus Collier (Frederick Forrester); Cecelia Henry (Lora Baxter); Richard Regan (William Gargan); Tom Collier (Leslie Howard); Franc Schmidt (Betty Lynne); Joe Fisk (Harvey Stephens); Daisy Sage (Katharine Hepburn, replaced by Frances Fuller after the Pittsburgh opening); Grace Macomber (Ilka Chase)
PRODUCED BY Gilbert Miller and Leslie Howard

1932

The Warrior's Husband (March, New York)
by Julian Thompson
DIRECTOR Burk Symon
CAST First Sergeant (Paula Bauersmith); Buria (Virginia Volland); Second Sergeant (Edna Holland); First Sentry (Frances Newbaker); Second Sentry (Avalon Plummer); Third Sentry (Rita Rheinfrank); Caustica (Bertha Belmore); Heroica (Dorothy Walters); Pomposia (Jane Wheatley); Hippolyta (Irby Marshal); Sapiens (Romney Brent); Sapiens Major (Arthur Bowyer); Antiope (Katharine Hepburn); Captain of Archers (Helene Fontaine); Theseus (Colin Keith-Johnston); Homer (Don Beddoe); Runner (Thelma Hardwick); Hercules (Al Ochs); Gaganius, the Herald (Porter Hall); Achilles (Alan Campbell); Ajax (Randolph Leymen); Amazon Sentries and Guards (Eleanor Goodrich, Nina Romano, Agnes George, Eve Bailey, Clara Waring, Dorothy Gillam and Rose Dresser); Amazon Huntresses (Theodosia Dusanne, Mary Stuart, Miriam Schiller and Barbara Dugan); Greek Warriors (Thaddeus Clancy, Walter Levin, Arthur Brady and Jerry Feigan)
PRODUCED BY Harry Moses

Summer Stock: Played Psyche Marbury in Will Cotton's *The Bride the Sun Shines On* for a stock company at Ossining, New York

1933

The Lake (December, New York)
by Dorothy Massingham and Murray MacDonald
DIRECTOR Jed Harris
CAST Mildred Surrege (Frances Starr); Williams (J. P. Wilson); Lena Surrege (Blanche Bates); Henry Surrege (Lionel Pape); Marjorie Hervey (Roberta Beatty); Stella Surrege (Katharine Hepburn); Ethel (Esther Mitchell); Cecil Hervey (Geoffrey Wardwell); John Clayne (Colin Clive); Maude (Mary Heberden); Stoker (Edward Broadley); Stephen Braite (Philip Tonge); Dotty Braite (Wendy Atkin); Jean Templeton (Audrey Ridgwell); Anna

George (Vera Fuller-Mellish); Mrs George (Rosalind Ivan); Miss Kurn (Florence Britton); Mrs Hemingway (Eva Leonard-Boyne); Dennis Gorlay (O. Z. Whitehead); Lady Stanway (Reginald Carrington); Captain Hamilton (James Grainger); Miss White (Lucy Beaumont); Lady Kerton (Elliott Mason)
PRODUCED BY Jed Harris

1936

Jane Eyre (December–April 1937, on tour)
by Charlotte Bronte, dramatised by Helen Jerome
DIRECTOR Worthington Miner
CAST Mrs Fairfax (Viola Roache); Leah (Phyllis Connard); Jane Eyre (Katharine Hepburn); Mr Rochester (Denis Hoey); Adele Varens (Patricia Peardon); Mason (Irving Morrow); Grace Poole (Teresa Dale); Blanche Ingram (Sandra Ellsworth); The Maniac (Teresa Guerini); Lady Ingram (Katharine Stewart); Lord Ingram (Reginald Carrington); Briggs (Wilfred Seagram); Rev Wood (Reginald Malcolm); Diana Rivers (Barbara O'Neil); Hannah (Marga Ann Deighton); St John Rivers (Stephen Kerr Appleby)
PRODUCED BY The Theatre Guild Inc.

1939

The Philadelphia Story (March, New York)
by Philip Barry
DIRECTOR Robert B. Sinclair
CAST Dinah Lord (Lenore Lonergan); Margaret Lord (Vera Allen); Tracy Lord (Katharine Hepburn); Alexander Lord (Dan Tobin); Thomas (Owen Coll); William Tracy (Forrest Orr); Elizabeth Imbrie (Shirley Booth); Macaulay Connor (Van Heflin); George Kittredge (Frank Fenton); C. K. Dexter Haven (Joseph Cotten); Edward (Philip Foster); Seth Lord (Nicholas Joy); May (Myrtle Tannahill); Elsie (Lorraine Bate); Mac (Hayden Rorke)
PRODUCED BY The Theatre Guild Inc.

1942

Without Love (November, New York and tour)
by Philip Barry
DIRECTOR Robert B. Sinclair
CAST Patrick Jamieson (Elliott Nugent); Quentin Ladd (Tony Bickley); Anna (Emily Massey); Martha Ladd (Ellen Morgan); Jamie Coe Rowan (Katharine Hepburn); Kitty Trimble (Audrey Christie); Peter Baillie (Robert Shayne); Paul Carrel (Sherling Oliver); Richard Hood (Robert Chisholm); Robert Emmet Riordan (Neil Fitzgerald); Grant Vincent (Royal Beal)
PRODUCED BY The Theatre Guild Inc.

1950

As You Like It (January, New York and tour)
by William Shakespeare
DIRECTOR Michael Benthall

CAST Orlando (William Prince); Adam (Burton Mallory); Oliver (Ernest Graves); Dennis (Robert Foster); Charles (Michael Everett); Celia (Cloris Leachman); Rosalind (Katharine Hepburn); Touchstone (Bill Owen); Le Beau (Jay Robinson); Frederick (Dayton Lummis); Lady in Waiting (Jan Sherwood); Duke (Aubrey Mather); Amiens (Frank Rogier); Lord (Everett Gamnon); Corin (Whitford Kane); Silvius (Robert Quarry); Phebe (Judy Parrish); Jaques (Ernest Thesiger); Audrey (Patricia Englund); Sir Oliver Martext (Jay Robinson); William (Robert Foster); Rowland (Craig Timberlake); Ladies in Waiting & Shepherdesses (Jan Sherwood, Marilyn Nowell, Margaret Wright); Lords, Attendants & Shepherds (Kenneth Cantril, Charles Herndon, William Sutherland, Richard Hepburn, Robert Wark, John Weaver, Craig Timberlake)
PRODUCED BY The Theatre Guild Inc.

1952

The Millionairess (June, New York and tour)
by George Bernard Shaw
DIRECTOR Michael Benthall
CAST Julius Sagamore (Campbell Cotts); Epifania, the Lady (Katharine Hepburn); Alastair Fitzfassenden (Peter Dyneley); Patricia Smith (Genine Graham); Adrain Blenderbland (Cyril Ritchard); The Doctor (Robert Helpmann); The Man (Bertram Shuttleworth); The Woman (Nora Nicholson); The Manager (Vernon Greeves)
PRODUCED BY Hugh Beaumont

1955

Summer Tour: Joined Robert Helpmann and the Old Vic Company to tour Australia as Portia in *The Merchant of Venice*; Katherina in *The Taming of the Shrew* and Isabella in *Measure for Measure*

1957

The Merchant of Venice (July, American Shakespeare Festival Theatre, Stratford, Connecticut)
by William Shakespeare
DIRECTOR Jack Landau
CAST Antonio (Richard Waring); Salerio (John Frid); Solanio (Kendall Clark); Bassanio (Donald Harron); Lorenzo (Richard Lupino); Gratiano (John Colicos); Portia (Katharine Hepburn); Nerissa (Lois Nettleton); Balthazar (Michael Kennedy); Shylock (Morris Carnovsky); Lancelot Gobbo (Richard Easton); Old Gobbo (William Cottrell); Prince of Morocco (Earle Hyman); Jessica (Dina Doronne); Prince of Arragon (Stanley Bell); Tubal (Jack Bittner); Stephano (Russell Oberlin); Duke of Venice (Larry Gates); Attendants, Citizens, Dignitaries (Conrad Bromberg, James Cahill, Richard Cavett, Harley Clements,

Tamara Daniel, Michael Kasdan, Simm Landres, Michele La Bombarda, Michael Lindsay-Hogg, Susan Lloyd, William Long Jr., Michael Miller, David Milton, Vivian Paszamont, Ira Rubin, D. J. Sullivan, Peter Trytler, Gail Warner

Much Ado About Nothing (August, American Shakespeare Festival Theatre, Stratford, Connecticut)
by William Shakespeare
DIRECTOR John Houseman and Jack Landau
CAST Borachio (Jack Bittner); Antonio (Morris Carnovsky); Balthazar (Russell Oberlin); Margaret (Sada Thompson); Ursula (Jacqueline Brookes); Dogberry (Larry Gates); Verges (Donald Harron); First Watchman (Richard Lupino); Second Watchman (William Cottrell); Friar Francis (Kendall Clark); Sexton (John Frid); Leonato (John Colicos); Messenger (Donald Harron); Beatrice (Katharine Hepburn); Hero (Lois Nettleton); Don Pedro (Stanley Bell); Benedick (Alfred Drake); Claudio (Richard Easton); Don John (Richard Waring); Conrade (Mitchell Agruss); Soldiers & Servants (Michael Bordern, Benita Deutsch, Michael Kasdan, Michael Miller, David Milton, Joe Myers, Dino Narizzano, Ira Rubin, Judith Steffan, Peter Trytler, Jack Waltzer, William Woodman)

1960

Twelfth Night (June, American Shakespeare Festival Theatre, Stratford, Connecticut)
by William Shakespeare
DIRECTOR Jack Landau
CAST Orsino, Duke of Illyria (Donald Davis); Curio (Stephen Strimpell); Valentine (John Harkins); Viola (Katharine Hepburn); A Sea Captain (Will Geer); Sir Toby Belch (Loring Smith); Maria (Sada Thompson); Sir Andrew Aguecheek (O. Z. Whitehead); Feste (Morris Carnovsky); Olivia (Margaret Phillips); Malvolio (Richard Waring); A Boy (David Gress); Fabian (William Hickey); Antonio (Clifton James); Sebastian (Clayton Corzatte); A Guardsman (Claude Woolman); Priest (Patrick Hines); Sailors, Fishermen, Guardsmen and Ladies (Constance Bollinger, Lorna Gilbert, Donald Hatch, Charles Herrick, Alfred Lavorato, George Parrish, Donald Pomes, Howard Poyrow, Robert Reilly, Lou Robb, Sandra Saget, George Sampson, Wisner Washam, Beverly Whitcomb)

Antony and Cleopatra (July, American Shakespeare Festival Theatre, Stratford.
by William Shakespeare
DIRECTOR Jack Landau
CAST Antony (Robert Ryan); Cleopatra (Katharine Hepburn); Canidius (Douglas Watson); Scarus (John Harkins); Enobarbus (Donald Davis); Mardian (Patrick Hines); Alexas (Earle Hyman); Charmian (Rae Allen); Iras (Anne Fielding); Octavius Caesar (John Ragin); Lepidus (Morris Carnovsky); Agrippa (Will

Geer); Thidius (John Myhers); Dolabella (Stephen Strimpell); Pompey (Clifton James); Menas (Claude Woolman); Octavia (Sada Thompson); A Soothsayer (Richard Waring); Egyptian Messenger (Ted Van Griethuysen); Eros (Clayton Corzatte); Officers, Soldiers, Attendants (John Abbey, Stephen Carnovsky, David Clayborne, Jack Gardner, David Groh, Donald Hatch, Charles Herrick, Lloyd Hezekiah, Joseph Kleinowski, Alfred Lavorato, Christopher Lloyd, Robert Packer, Christian Parker, George Parrish, Don Pomes, Howard Poyrow, Robert Reilly, Lou Robb, George Sampson, Frank Spencer, Richard Thayer, Herman Tucker, Wisner Washam)

1969

Coco (December, New York and tour)
book and lyrics by Alan Jay Lerner
music by André Previn
DIRECTOR Michael Benthall
CAST Helene (Maggie Task); Pignol (Jeanne Arnold); Armand (Al DeSio); A Seamstress (Nancy Killmer); Albert (Jack Beaber); A Lawyer (Richard Marr); Louis Greff (George Rose); Docaton (Eve March); Coco (Katharine Hepburn); Georges (David Holliday); Loublaye (Gene Varrone); Varne (Shirley Potter); Marie (Lynn Winn); Jeanine (Rita O'Connor); Claire (Graciela Daniele); Juliette (Margot Travers); Madelaine (Carolyn Kirsch); Lucille (Diane Phillips); Simone (Charlene Ryan); Solange (Suzanne Rogers); Noelle (Gale Dixon); Sebastian Baye (Rene Auberjonois); Dr Petitjean (Richard Woods); Claude (David Thomas); Dwight Berkwit (Will B. Able); Eugene Bernstone (Robert Fitch); Ronny Ginsborn (Chad Block); Phil Rosenberry (Dan Siretta); Lapidus (Gene Varrone); Nadine (Leslie Daniel); Grand Duke (Jack Dabdoub); Charles (Michael Allinson); Julian Lesage (Paul Dumont); Papa (Jon Cypher)
PRODUCED BY Frederick Brisson

1976

A Matter of Gravity (February, New York and tour)
by Enid Bagnold
DIRECTOR Noel Willman
CAST Mrs Basil (Katharine Hepburn), with Charlotte Jones, Christopher Reeve, Paul Harding, Wanda Bimson and Elizabeth Lawrence
PRODUCED BY Robert Whitehead, Roger L. Stevens and Konrad Matthaei

1981

The West Side Waltz (November, New York and tour)
by Ernest Thompson
DIRECTOR Noel Willman
CAST Margaret Elderdice (Katharine Hepburn), with Dorothy Loudon, David Margulies, Regina Baff, Don Howard
PRODUCED BY Robert Whitehead and Roger L. Stevens

ACKNOWLEDGEMENTS

The following illustrations appear by the kind
permission of: Cecil Beaton, courtesy of Sothebys,
London: p. 24, 85, 126, 192; Bison Archives: p. 66/
67; Ben Carbonetto: p. 31, 37, 56, 57, 61, 92
(middle), 102 (bottom), 103, 130, 131, 138 (top and
bottom left), 139, 154, 167 (bottom), 172; Culver
Pictures Inc: p. 19, 28, 29; John Hillelson: p. 191;
Hurrell: p. 91, courtesy of The Kobal Collection;
Cornel Lucas: p. 2; Museum of Modern Art: p. 18,
20, 76 (left), 134, 167 (top); New York Public
Library: p. 26; Phototeque: p. 122; Springer/
Betteman Film Archive: p. 21; John Topham:
p. 154/155; UPI/Betteman: p. 27, 128, 156/157.

The author would like to thank Sally Hibbin for her
invaluable research.

The publishers acknowledge with thanks the
cooperation of the following.
Columbia, RKO, MGM, United Artists,
Paramount, Twentieth Century Fox, Embassy,
Warner Brothers, ITC, Ben Carbonetto, Mary
Corliss and Mark Wanamaker.